A Tribute to Paula Aldersley

We wish to record our very deep appreciation of the administrative work which Paula has done for the Initiative over the past two years. It was a great shock to us all to learn, in August, of Paula's death at the very early age of 25.

Since the death of William Gowland, the Initiative's founder, when the Initiative's Office was established in Plymouth, Paula took on the clerical workload and in that time has administratively enabled the Initiative to find its new feet. Paula became known to many, not only through the regular mailings, but also at the Consultation in Oxford last April.

Our prayers and kind thoughts go to Paula's husband, Paul, and to her two daughters Gemma and Hannah.

ISBN 0 9514482 7 7

Being Human in a Cosmic Context

The 7th "Christ & the Cosmos" Publication

> *Let your bearing towards one another arise out of your life in Christ Jesus. For the divine nature was his from the first; yet he did not think to snatch at equality with God, but made himself nothing, assuming the nature of a slave. Bearing the human likeness, revealed in human shape, he humbled himself, and in obedience accepted death -even death on a cross. Therefore God raised him to the height and bestowed on him the name above all names, that at the name of Jesus every knee should bow - in heaven, on earth, and in the depths -and every tongue confess, 'Jesus Christ is Lord', to the glory of God the Father.*
>
> *Philippians 2:5-11 (NEB)*

Others in the series:

"Christ and the Cosmos" : (1987)

"Christ and the Cosmos" : Volume II (1989)

"Christ and the Cosmos" : Volume III (1990)

"Christ and the Cosmos" : Mission and Complexity (1991)

"Christ and the Cosmos" : Interpreting the Cosmos (1992)

and

"Taking the Initiative" : (March, 1993)

Being Human in a Cosmic Context
Volume VII in the "Christ & the Cosmos" Series

A report on the Conference held
at Westminster College, Oxford
from 2nd to 4th April, 1993

LECTURERS and PREACHER

Professor David Booth, M.A., Ph.D., D.Sc., C.Psychol., F.B.Ps.S.

Rt. Rev. Richard Harries, M.A.

Dr. John Sloper, M.A., D.Phil., B.M., B.Ch., F.R.C.S.

Rev. Dr. David Wilkinson, B.Sc., Ph.D., B.A., F.R.A.S.

Rev. David Winter, B.A.

Rev. Professor Frances Young, B.A., M.A., Ph.D.

Initiative Officers and 1993 Organising Panel

Chairman	Mr John Barratt, LL.M.
Editor	Rev. Stuart Roebuck, B.D., F.C.I.I.
Secretary	Mrs Margaret Barrett
Chaplain	Rev. Edgar Daniel
Treasurer	Mr Peter Cannell, D.L.C., F.Inst.P.S.
1993 Co-ordinator	Mr Ron Glithero, B.A., B.D.
Panel Members	Dr. K. Bertie Everard, B.Sc, Ph.D.,F.R.S.A.
	Dr. Richard Hooker, B.Sc., Ph.D.
	Mr David Peck, B.Sc.

Publication Team

Editor	Rev. Stuart Roebuck, B.D., F.C.I.I.
Sound Recording	Mr. Rowland Budgen, M.Phil., B.Ed., F.I.M.L.S., M.I.Biol.
Copy Preparation	Rev. Gordon James, B.A.

PUBLISHED BY

The Christ and the Cosmos Initiative
and
Westminster College, Oxford

Readers' comments and enquiries on this book or about the Initiative in general will be welcomed.

Please write to any member of the Panel, or simply to

'The Christ and the Cosmos Initiative', care of the Chaplain's Office, Wesley Church, The Crescent, PLYMOUTH, PL1 3AB

Foreward

Mrs. Margaret Gowland

At the seventh Annual Consultation of the Christ and the Cosmos Initiative I was honoured with the title of Honorary President. I gladly accepted it in memory of Bill's endeavours to initiate this project.

When Bill retired from the active Methodist Ministry, he spent most of his days in his study -reading, researching and contacting people. His main objective was to interest and encourage folk to participate in his vision and venture. That is how it all started -sheer determination to make it work. I believe that that determination is still inspiring the Panel and its helpers.

They have worked hard in so many ways, including preparing this excellent 7th Consultation Programme which we all enjoyed. In the early days Mrs Margaret Barrett worked with Bill in the office and still continues with some administration today. I should like to offer her my personal thanks for her loyalty and continual support. I am grateful too for the progress which has been accomplished by individual members and friends of the Initiative. They have given splendid support over the past years.

I suggested at the beginning of the 7th Consultation that we were about to have a challenging and thought-provoking weekend, and that proved to be so. We were very grateful to all the lecturers for their contributions -for the knowledge and understanding of God's universe which they shared with us. In our devotions too, we were spiritually and socially inspired, which gave an extra depth of meaning to the weekend.

Nearly every week a new theory or revelation of the universe is exposed. Our greatest hopes can become reality if we keep on questioning and enquiring about the sovereign power of God and his universe.

In the words of the hymn by Albert Bayley and Brian Wren:

Lord of the boundless curves of space

And time's deep mystery,

To your creative might we trace

All nature's energy.

(Hymns & Psalms 335)

Introduction

In case this is the first time you have opened one of our publications, let's begin by telling again the story of how the *Christ and the Cosmos* Initiative came into being.

The Story so far

It started with an idea, as most really important things do. The thinker was Bill Gowland, a Methodist Minister of renown. He had founded Luton Industrial College in the 1950s. He was President of the Methodist Conference in 1979. And he had retired reluctantly at the age of 75 in 1986.

For many years he had been aware that science and religion seemed to be two opposites in the eyes of many people. He did not share that belief. He knew that there were many scientists who were also Christians and who did not share it either. So he invited about fifty of his friends to meet for a weekend near Easter in 1987. The group comprised mainly scientists, theologians, and people involved in education. It was a tremendously exciting and stimulating weekend, remembered with affection by the people who were there. The group realised that they were on to something important and that the work had only just begun.

A report (we prefer to call it a book) was produced which contained the weekend's lectures, discussion group findings, specially-written articles, a study plan, a bibliography and so on. It sold very widely. The following Spring another weekend conference was held. Interest was maintained. The *Initiative* came into being. And as the years have gone by it has grown considerably.

The *Christ and the Cosmos Initiative* is a loose association of people who are interested in the relationship between science and religion. It attracts men and women of any age, any background, any religious affiliation or none. At its heart is the knowledge that what science has had to say has been the breaking point of religious faith for many people in recent generations. Science is challenging, exciting, rewarding, bold, adventurous, forward-looking. Religion by comparison often seems not merely dull, uninspired, amateurish, irrelevant and old-fashioned, but actually wrong. The Initiative seeks to carry forward the mission of the Church by showing that there is no necessary conflict between science and religion, but that both are in the business of revelation. The Initiative keeps on asking the question: "What has science revealed which might make a difference to our theology or the way we express it?"

The *Initiative's* methods of looking at this question are simple. The *Springtime weekend conferences* have continued to thrive, about a hundred people meeting at Westminster College, Oxford, each year; some people have been to every conference, but there are always new faces as well. Each conference has been followed by a book which we have tried to sell as widely as possible. During the past three years one day or half a day regional conferences have been held in many parts of the country, usually because of the enthusiasm of our supporters who live in these regions. The *Initiative's publications* have been used in series of discussions in Preachers' Meetings, Fellowship Groups and the like. And we are particularly indebted to the **Methodist Recorder** which has been unfailing in its support by reporting our activities to a wide circle of readers.

A New Initiative

In March 1993 a new kind of book was produced. It is called '*Taking the Initiative*'. About two thirds of the book comprises representative extracts from all our previous publications and from some specially written papers. The other one third is made up of explanations and introductions to matters of specific interest in the science / religion debate. Each of its many sections is followed by questions to help study groups to get to grips with the issues raised. '*Taking the Initiative*' may be regarded as the Initiative's textbook for the next few years. It is obtainable by post from our Chaplain's Office in Plymouth for £7 plus £1 packing and posting.

Spring 1993

That brings us up to date. In fact, to the conference which gave rise to the book you are holding. It was held as usual at Westminster College. It ran from the evening of Friday 2nd April to just after lunch on Sunday 4th April. It was an excellent conference with splendid speakers, an opportunity to renew friendships and make new ones.

An opening event was of great pleasure to everyone. Mrs Margaret Gowland kindly agreed to become Honorary President of the Initiative, following in the steps of her husband. We are grateful that she has written the Foreword to this book.

Each year we wonder how we can possibly maintain the standard next year, yet we always have and the conferences have always been tremendously worthwhile. Plans are already well in hand for the 1994 conference. It will run at the same times of day from 8th to 10th of April. The theme will concern the well-being of the earth, 'Being Responsible in a Cosmic Context'. The lecturers will include a geographer, a material scientist, two professors of theology, a government chief scientist and a President of the Law Society. Booking details are available from the office in Plymouth.

The theme in 1993 was human existence, 'Being Human in a Cosmic Context'. The lectures followed a natural progression. We began with a reflection about knowledge, then worked from the basics of biological existence to the brain and mind, then to the human in society, to human aesthetic appreciation, and finally to the human spirit. The lectures are all given in this book, together with reports on the question and answer sessions which followed them.

Thanks are due to all who play a part in planning and organising our conferences, both well in advance and actually during the weekends.
Thanks to members of the organising panel, chairmen and secretaries of

discussion groups, those who chair lectures or sell books, and people who welcome us to Westminster College, including the Principal, the Rev. Dr Kenneth B. Wilson, and his Staff. Special thanks to Mr Rowland Budgen without whose recordings of lectures it would have been impossible to write this book, and to Rev. Gordon James whose desktop publishing skills are enabling us to produce books at a professional standard.

Comments from readers will be appreciated, addressed to any of us at the office in Plymouth.

Biographical Notes on the Lecturers

Professor David Booth, M.A., Ph.D., D.Sc., C.Psychol., F.B.Ps.S.

David Booth comes from a missionary family and was schooled in natural science from the age of 10. His Ph.D. is in brain chemistry, but in his first term in Birmingham reading chemistry a fellow student introduced him to experimental psychology and analytical philosophy. He took a second degree in those subjects at Birkbeck College, University of London, primarily out of a Christian interest. He then went into psychological research both in the U.S.A., and at Sussex University, before talking a permanent post at Birmingham, where he obtained a D.Sc. for research papers in psychology.

Professor Booth is currently Research Group Co-ordinator in Nutritional Psychology in the School of Psychology, University of Birmingham. He sees Initiatives such as the Christ and the Cosmos Initiative as being among the media of redemption for our time.

Rt. Rev. Richard Harries, M.A.

Richard Harries has been Bishop of Oxford since 1987, having previously served as Dean of King's College, University of London, from 1981. He was on the staff of Wells Theological College from 1969 to 1972, and as Vicar of All Saints, Fulham, from 1972 to 1981.

He is a man of wide interests and concerns. Consultant to the Archbishop of Canterbury on Jewish-Christian relations, he is the author of a number of books, particularly on prayer and on Christian concerns in contemporary society. He is a frequent broadcaster.

Dr. John Sloper, M.A., D.Phil., B.M., B.Ch., F.R.C.S.

John Sloper qualified in medicine and subsequently spent eleven years in research into the structure of the brain in the Anatomy Department of the University of Oxford on visual systems. During this research he was awarded his D.Phil.. He then trained as an eye surgeon, to become

Ophthalmic Registrar at the Royal Victoria Hospital, Belfast. He has published a number of papers on this particular field of work.

Dr. Sloper has recently returned to England to take up his new position of Senior Registrar in the Eye Department, Queen's Medical Centre, University of Nottingham.

Rev. Dr. David A. Wilkinson, B.Sc., Ph.D., B.A., F.R.A.S.

David Wilkinson studied for his first degree in physics at Durham, where he also gained his Ph.D. in theoretical astrophysics. His research in astrophysics has included studies of star formation, the chemical evolution of galaxies and terrestrial mass extinctions. He is a Fellow of the Royal Astronomical Society. While training for the Methodist Ministry in Cambridge he completed a degree in Theology.

At present he is serving as Methodist Minister at Elm Hall Drive Methodist Church, Liverpool, and as Methodist Chaplain to Liverpool University. One of his continuing concerns is the relation of modern cosmology to natural theology and the creation/evolution debate. In addition to heavy ministerial duties he is now given time by the church to continue work on the relationship of science and Christianity.

Rev. David Winter, B.A.

Former school teacher, editor and freelance writer and broadcaster, David Winter worked in B.B.C. Radio from the early 1970s, becoming Head of Religious Programmes, B.B.C. Radio in 1982. From 1987 to 1989 he was Head of Religious Broadcasting for the B.B.C.

Following ordination he has been priest-in-charge of Ducklington in Oxfordshire and the Bishop's Officer for Evangelism which involves him in much travelling and activity in the diocese. He continues his active interest in religious broadcasting and journalism.

Rev. Professor Frances Young, B.A., M.A., Ph.D.

Educated at Bedford College, University of London, and Girton College, Cambridge, Frances Young was appointed to the staff of Birmingham University in 1971. In 1986 she became the Edward Cadbury Professor of Theology. Her published works include 'Sacrifice and the Death of Christ' (1975), 'Face to Face' (revised edition 1990), 'Focus on God' - with Kenneth Wilson (1986), and 'The Art of Performance' (1990).

Ordained into the Methodist ministry in 1984, Professor Young, in addition to her strenuous academic activity, serves in the Birmingham West Circuit, preaches regularly, and is a regular columnist in the Methodist Recorder.

Part One:
LECTURES AND QUESTION SESSIONS

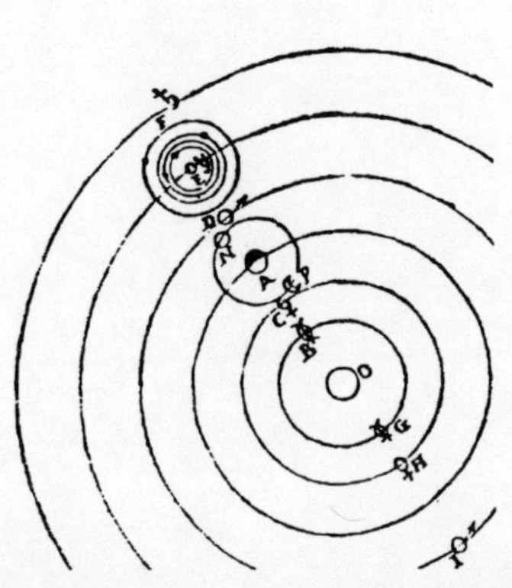

How do we know what we think we know?

Rev. Dr. David Wilkinson

Thank you for the privilege of inviting me to speak at an Initiative Consultation for a second time. I was encouraged to be part of the Initiative by Bill Gowland in his inimitable way, and it is nice to be part of this programme.

I don't feel, however, that the title which I've been given for this lecture is particularly nice! I feel like the eccentric millionaire who used to hold parties by his swimming pool. In the pool there was a man-eating shark. At one of the parties he said, "If anyone has enough courage to jump in at one end and swim to the other, I'll give him half my money or half my land or the hand of my beautiful daughter in marriage." Suddenly there was a splash at one end of the pool. A man was seen swimming with all his strength to the other end and he got out just in time. The millionaire was amazed. "That was incredible," he said, "Do you want half my money?" "No:" replied the man. "Do you want half my land?" "No," again. "Do you want the hand of my daughter in marriage?" "No," came the reply again. "Then what do you want?" said the millionaire. "I just want to know," said the man, "who pushed me in?"

The title of this lecture makes me feel like that swimmer. By training I'm a physicist rather than a philosopher or a social scientist. I welcome very much the direction of the Consultation this year. I think the theme is splendid. But a physicist by training follows Lord Rutherford's comment that all science is physics and stamp-collecting. Therefore, since I'm not very knowledgeable about philosophy and the social sciences, a lot of what I'll say will come from my background of physics.

How do we know what we think we know? It's an interesting question. Some people will immediately say, "It's obvious." Others will say, "I don't even understand the question." The first point with such a title is to remember that the verb 'to know' is used in different senses. "I know that two plus two equals four," is quite different from saying "I know .... somebody else."

Richard Feynman, the great theoretical physicist, as a young child was often taken by his father for nature walks in the local woods. After one of these walks another small boy came and said to him, "Tell me, what's the name of that bird?" Feynman didn't know. The other boy said, "You mean your father takes you for nature walks, but he doesn't even tell you the name of that bird?" Feynman was upset. He said to his father, "Why didn't you tell me the name of that bird?" "Well," said his father, "In English it's called ...., in Chinese it's ....., in Arabic...., in French ...., in German ...... You might know the name of the bird in all the languages around the world, but that won't tell you what kind of an environment it needs in order to survive. You won't understand how it breeds, feeds and develops."

There are many ways of using the verb 'to know', but what I'm going to concentrate on this evening is perceiving or understanding truth in the scientific sense and in the theological sense.

First, a very famous quotation from Bertrand Russell:

> We have to ask ourselves whether in any sense at all there is such a thing as matter. Is there a table which has a certain intrinsic nature and continues to exist when I'm not looking, or is it that the table is merely a product of my imagination, a dream table in a very prolonged dream? The question is of the greatest importance, for if we cannot be sure of the independent existence of objects, we cannot be sure of the independent existence of other people's bodies; and therefore still less of other people's minds, since we have no grounds for believing in their minds except such as are derived from observing their bodies. Thus if we cannot be sure of the independent existence of objects, we shall be left alone in a desert. It may be that the whole outer world is nothing but a dream and that we alone exist.
>
> [Bertrand Russell, 'The Problems of Philosophy', OUP, New York, (1912), p. 17]

How do we really know that something exists out there? This whole area of though goes under the philosophical name of epistemology, the study of the possibility and nature of knowledge. John Pollock writes:

> The fundamental problem of epistemology is to explain what it is that justifies us making the kinds of knowledge claims that we customarily make.
>
> [J. Pollock, 'Knowledge and Justification', Princeton University Press, Princeton, (1974), p.7]

What is the relationship between matter and mind? As an anonymous author wrote:

> "What is matter? Never mind. What is mind? It doesn't matter."

Now that's the type of question we are going to look at this evening. What I'd like to do is to look first at how we know what we think we know in science and then in theology, and then try to draw some things together.

The popular image of how we know things is often very different whether you talk about it in the scientific context or in the theological context in modern society. Mark Twain wrote:

> There's something fascinating about science. One gets such a wholesome return of conjecture out of such a trifling investment of fact.

Such scepticism is quite unusual, because the popular image of science is an ever-increasing ability to explain, to know, to understand. Science is viewed as extremely successful. It is the authority that people look to. It gives explanations for those things which were once thought to be the realm of religion. If we were looking for a parable or model of modern science, it would be Mr Spock in Star Trek. It seems that anything is possible for him by the combination of a little logic, a little science, and a big enough computer. You can discover what has happened in the past, what will happen in the future and everything else. From the evolution of the universe to the origin of life and the evolution of species -science has something to say. But more than that. Science itself seems to give the impression that once it has said something, there is nothing more to say about it. Modern technology, whether it is determining the sex of a child or operating a Super Nintendo Game Boy, encourages us in believing that the world is easily manipulated by our understanding of science.

Theology, of course, is much different in the popular imagination. One is dogmatic belief, despite the evidence, the fundamentalist view, where faith becomes, in the schoolboy definition, 'believing those things you know aren't true'. The other extreme is a kind of wittering unsure uncertain description of the world in language that no one can understand. I was once in a room with some physicists listening to a certain bishop on the television, who said, "I should have thought that in my position, I wouldn't have said what you've said I've said, which I do not believe I have said, though not as clearly as you said it ...." which was his attempt to say "Yes"! The way that group of physicists viewed what he said was quite illuminating!

So I want to look at these two areas and to see whether the popular mythology about them is true or not.

How do we know what we think we know in science?

1. By reason alone?

First let me take a popular view. Is it by reason alone? Is science all about making calculations on the back of an envelope with a pencil? Many of you will have read Stephen Hawking's book 'A Brief History of Time'. A famous book, it has sold more copies that 'A Diary of an Edwardian Country Lady'. What is fascinating about the cover is the blackboard in the background covered in long equations. Hawking himself doesn't actually use a blackboard, but that is the popular image of a great scientist, deriving the whole history of the universe with a blackboard and a piece of chalk by pure thought.

It's an image by which some people characterise Greek science, the way of looking for elegance or beauty and then building a view of the cosmos out of that. The Greek view gave rise to what many of you will know as Ptolemy's view of the solar system. From Aristotle's belief in the beauty of circles, which indeed we see in the circular movement of the night sky, Ptolemy saw that some of the stars do not move in clear circles as the others do, but that for some there is retrograde motion. He explained that by the imposition of circle upon circle.

Such rationalism by reason alone was also found in philosophy. For example, Descartes doubting everything until he worked to just "I think therefore I am", in his attempt to build a view of the world on absolutely certain starting premises, then by logic deriving an absolutely certain view of the world. Of course, it doesn't work. Where do you get certain starting points? Mathematicians here will know that Godel's theorem says that certain statements even within mathematics can be stated but not proved. The way of reason alone falls down in contact with the real world.

I receive a number of manuscripts these days. Some of them are very detailed, of thesis length, on new views of the universe. I received one the other day called 'Astro-physics and Sex: A New Synthesis'. Another one was a 300-page thesis which derived the origin of the universe from certain starting premises about circles in geometry. The trouble was that there were several mistakes on page one in terms of observation which invalidated everything else. Reason alone is not the way that science proceeds.

There is a story of some mathematicians who were employed by the Milk Marketing Board to help them with the production and distribution of milk. The mathematicians' report was rejected; it began with the words,

"Suppose we begin with a circular cow." Pure rationalism doesn't always relate to life! George Gamov the astrophysicist said that any mathematician worth his salt could derive the profile of an elephant if he had five free parameters. You can do that by reason alone, but it doesn't actually relate to the real world.

2. By Data Alone?

So the second view is not of a scientist sitting down with a pencil and paper, but of a scientist gazing benignly at the night sky or sitting in a bath and saying, "Eureka!" The observations lead to the understanding. The importance of data or Western empiricism. The ability to look at the Universe and from our observations to derive an understanding of it.

Of course, it is true that the observations in science are very important. Galileo revolutionised astronomy by pointing his telescope at the moons of Jupiter. Some people have argued that it was the intervention of the Christian world view into the intellectual concept of the day that gave the main impetus for the rise of 17th Century science. As God had made the universe as a free act, we had to observe the universe to deduce its nature. As God was a God of order, there would be scientific laws. As we are made in the image of God, we would have some hope of understanding these laws. And as there is only one God, we expected that the laws of physics would be consistent throughout the universe. I think some people have overplayed this interpretation, but nevertheless it was one of the most important factors in the growth of what we would call modern science. Indeed the Reformation helped by freeing the intellect from the grip of some dogmatic assertions, and enabled Galileo and his followers down the centuries to plot the course of modern science.

But the trouble is that such a view of science simply getting what it knows by looking and then drawing out an immediate theory, just doesn't work. It doesn't work for a number of reasons.

The first is that sometimes data can be interpreted two ways or it changes with time. Two years ago I showed you a photograph of the temperature of the microwave background of the universe across the whole sky, taken by COBE, a NASA satellite, in May 1990. The point I made was that the data was giving a lot of problems. It was colour-coded to show temperature, amazingly showing the universe as all the same temperature with the exception of our own galaxy. Two years ago I felt that this should not be the case. If galaxies form in the universe, the temperature of the microwave background should vary. Last Easter, however, the map changed. COBE had looked at things more closely. We now saw that there were 'ripples' in the universe, and what we saw was not uniform temperature but little patches which were claimed to be the seeds of galaxies as we look back into time. The trouble is that other scientists using the same data would disagree, saying that the ripples are not indications of seeds of galaxy formation, but are more local effects to our own galaxy. Sometimes data can be viewed in two ways.

The second problem with the 'by data alone' view is that often in the history of science it has been by the interplay of observation and theory that things have gone well. That is particularly the case in terms of the Big Bang theory. In the 1940s theoreticians looking at the origin of the Big Bang said that the Big Bang would produce about 25% helium in the universe. It wasn't until the late 1980s, when we were able to look at the universe with sophisticated instruments, that we were able to see that the universe does in fact have approximately 25% helium. That is a good example of the way in which science has an interplay between theory and observation. Experience and interpretation. Isaac Newton didn't get gravity just from an apple falling on his head, he needed interpretation of the apple's falling, too. Theory needed to go hand - in - hand with observation.

The third problem with the only - data approach is, what makes a good theory? On a purely data basis for many years there was no difference between Ptolemy and Copernicus in their view of the universe. But scientists use criteria and make judgements on what is a good theory, not just on data. They talk about elegance, simplicity, fruitfulness, unifying power, consistency with other theories which encourages you to believe that your theory is better than the other one. That was part of the reason why Copernicus triumphed over Ptolemy.

3. So what is science?

So if what we have said is that it's not by reason alone, and it's not by data alone, what is science? I'm sure we would all agree that science is the attempt by observation of the world to look for patterns by which the complexity of the universe can be understood. Then, however, we might have a disagreement on what science achieves. I'm going to suggest to you that there are five ways of viewing the achievement of science.

a) Naive realism: Most scientists in my experience view science in this way, the belief that the models or theories of science give a literal description of the world as it is. So when I talk about a model like the Big Bang, I'm speaking about what actually happened. The trouble with that is, what happens when we have two theories current in the scientific community? What about the fact that theories do change? Someone once said that cosmologists are never in doubt but are always in error. Einstein did come along and contradict Newton's view that mass doesn't change, by saying that, as a body travels at greater and greater velocity nearer the speed of light, the mass increases. How do we cope with that if it's naive realism?

In addition, what about this awful thing called 'quantum theory'? The classic experiment in quantum theory is to have a source of electrons and a screen which has two holes in it. If you pass the source of electrons through this arrangement, what you build up on a television screen to detect them is a pattern. As a number of electrons arrive, it builds up into a fringe pattern with peaks and troughs. If you close one of the holes so that the beam of electrons goes through only one hole, the pattern is quite different. The nice thing about this experiment is that you can choose how many electrons you want to send through the the arrangement. You can get down to sending just one electron through. The fascinating thing about it is that, if you send one electron through the two - hole experiment, it will fall within the two - hole pattern. If you send one electron through the one - hole arrangement, it will fall within the one - hole pattern. Now, you may say, how does the electron in the first one, if it passes through one hole, actually know there is another hole there? It's a fundamental question. Most physicists are agreed that there's no answer to it. The only possible answer is that this electron seems to go through both holes. But in our common everyday experience, if I go out of this room, I must go through one door or the other: I cannot go through both. At the quantum level that which is unimaginable in everyday terms becomes the only thing that we can say. The simple point I want to make is that here is a fundamental theory of physics which doesn't describe everything in naive literal everyday terms. And therefore I suggest that naive realism in terms of one's view of science is not the best way to look at it.

b) Positivism: This sees science as simply telling stories about effects in measuring instruments. It simply says that, when I see light from a distant galaxy, all science is about is telling the story of what happens in the measuring instruments either of my eyes or of my telescope. Those of you who are trained in philosophy will know that positivism as a philosophical theory has undergone a certain demise, but in one sense a view of science like this is rather ludicrous. So to say that, when Edwin Hubble saw the red shift of galaxies, all he was doing was seeing certain fringes move on his measuring instruments and that it had no relation to the universe, seems to be a ludicrous way of viewing science.

c) Instrumentalism: Whenever I speak to engineers I always come a cropper, because as pure scientists we have slightly different views of what science is about. Speaking to a group the other day, an engineer said to me, "I'm not interested in what science explores. The only thing I'm interested in is how I can use it in order to exploit the world." That's fair enough if you are an engineer. The trouble is that some people will say that this is all that science is, that science is simply a way of attempting to exploit or control the world. It seems to me that once again this is a ludicrous view of science. It is like saying that we put men on the moon in order to invent non - stick frying pans. It denies the basic human attitude of curiosity, of saying, "How does it work?" We want to ask these questions for their own sake. That's what science is about.

d) Idealism: It stems from the philosophy of Immanuel Kant. It sees science as a function of the way our minds organise the data of our senses. The order of the physical laws does not exist in nature, but is imposed onto nature by our minds. Science does not give knowledge of the world in itself, rather it shows us how our minds work. To follow an illustration of John Polkinghorne, it's rather like trawling the sea for fish with a net that has 4 inch holes in it. At the end of your trawl when you analyse the length of the fish, you not conclude that fish smaller than 4 inches do not exist. That order you have imposed onto that which you are exploring by the nature of what you are doing.

Idealism would say that our minds do that. It might be worth saying that, following this kind of philosophy, there has come into being a whole school of human knowledge, the sociology of knowledge school, in which people have argued that science is socially produced, rather than coming from any objective reality underneath.

Now, of course, such anti-realist views -and I've probably lumped together positivism, instrumentalism and idealism - are very fashionable, often with philosophers of science rather than scientists themselves. There is some truth, of course, about the human element in our knowing with which social sciences have helped us. There is the strange phenomenon of the role of the observer in the quantum theory. And the fact that theories do change. However, I want to say that such an anti-realist view of science must be dismissed. As John Barrows has said, "It is a glove which is very fashionable, but it is ill-fitting." It doesn't fit with the history or the present day experience of science.

Britain has invested £50 million in the William Hershel telescope in the Canary Islands. If the science which is being done there has no technological spin-offs, and is simply telling the story of what is happening in the measuring instruments or what the human mind is imposing on the universe, it all seems to me a waste of money. Psychologists would be much cheaper! I suggest there is something about the nature of science which is about exploring objective reality. Theories do change, but there is continuity between theories. Einstein has to explain Newton at speeds slower than the speed of light. Idealism in particular has a bad track record. For example, Immanuel Kant believed from his study of human knowledge that the universe had a certain geometry. We know that it has a different geometry. He was totally wrong.

Furthermore, I think those of us who have been scientists will testify to the very odd experience of reality poking its head through our thick skulls. In 1965 Arno Pensias and Robert Wilson were doing an experiment with microwaves. They weren't all interested in the Big Bang. They picked up a static on their sets. They couldn't get rid of it. They thought it was pigeon droppings, but it wasn't. It was the microwave background radiation of the universe, a fundamental piece of evidence for the Big Bang. Reality has a way of poking its head through our stubborn ideas. The surprising things about it is that it is often more subtle and simple than we would expect. There is a real feeling of discovery and surprise.

Well, is there any way of holding together what we have seen is wrong with 'by reason alone' and 'by data alone', and what is wrong with anti - realism? I think there is, and this is the last one which leads on to the definition which I will propose.

e) Critical realism: This I believe is the correct view of how we know what we think we know in science. It is realism in the sense that it takes seriously what our sense data and scientific instruments do tell us about reality. Huxley said that science was characterised by its humility before the facts. There is something out there, and all theories are fact-laden.

However, it is 'critical' for three reasons. First, our description of the everyday world is not always a literal everyday description. That's the point of quantum theory.

Second, there are personal judgements that we make within science. How many of you remember in school physics plotting a graph of two variables, x against y, when doing an experiment? Inevitably what what you want to get out of it is a number of points which lie on a straight line. A number of your points do so, but one stands apart. Now, you don't necessarily have to do the whole experiment again. There could be several explanations why the odd point doesn't lie on the line. One might be that you were distracted while doing the experiment and made a mistake. Another may be that there in 3rd form physics you had discovered a whole new theory of the universe and the odd point was correct. The way you decide which it is involves personal judgements -what conditions were prevailing, how significant the errors are, how significant the other points are. In science there is a weighing of the evidence which involves personal judgements.

Michael Polanyi in a famous book called 'Personal Knowledge' talked about 'tacit skills' -personal judgements that are made in science on what is worth doing, how you go from a limited amount of data to propose a theory, the problem of induction, the aspect of science which involves creative imagination. It is said of Kekule, the great chemist, that when he was trying to work out the structure of benzene, he became so tired that he started to fall asleep in front of a fire, and as he did so he had a vision of a snake grasping its own tail, and suddenly hit on the idea that benzene is a ring of carbon atoms joined together. He then, of course, had to go and test the theory by experiment, but this story illustrates that there is a place for creative imagination and intuition within the process of science as part of tacit skills.

All this is done within the limiting of the scientific community by referees' reports on papers and what is taught to generation after generation. But what I'm arguing here is that personal judgements cannot be made by computers. Science is ultimately a human enterprise. A survey on accidents found that 90% of accidents on stairs happen on the top or bottom stair, That was fed into a computer which was then asked how accidents could be reduced. The computer replied "Remove the top and bottom stair". So I'm very hesitant about the induction principles of Francis Bacon and John Stuart Mill which suggest that there is a regimented way to do science. It is much more messy in terms of the role of the human in science.

Thirdly, theories exhibit not absolute literal truth but what some philosophers of science would call 'verisimilitude'. I'm sorry there are many such words in this lecture. But that word means what it sounds like, that is 'very similar to'. That's what scientific theories are about. They are always improving, giving a tightening grip on objective reality.

So how do we know what we think we know in science? This has been a long torrid way of answering the question, but I have tried to map out some of the ground. My answer is:

> We know what we think we know by the subtle interplay of experience and interpretation involving personal judgements in a committed community exploring an objective reality.

That may ring some bells, if you are a theologian, and that is what we are going to move onto next. I want to ask, if that is truly what science is about, what in theology would be the similarities and differences?

How do we know what we think we know in theology?

Obviously, people like Ian Barbour and John Polkinghorne have done this in a far more detailed way than I can. Similarities with science? First, theology does not proceed by reason alone. The logical proofs of the existence of God, particularly the ontological proof, just do not quite work. Although there has been a revival of some of the classical arguments for the existence of God, which may be pointers rather than proofs, I would argue that by reason alone theology does not proceed.

Second, as in science, I believe that in theology there are pieces of evidence or data, something is given with which to explore. For example, the kind of experience of the numinous as described by Rudolph Otto, or by Peter Berger's ideas in 'Signals of Transcendence', or the Alister Hardy Research Centre's discoveries which say that over 60% of people have some kind of religious experience. There is a givenness of religious experience which theology needs to explore, whether it be a sense of awe or guilt, of forgiveness or peace. Also there are historical events. One of the original meanings of the word Gospel is 'epoch-making event'. As a physicist I like the word event. It is something I see in a cloud chamber and can look at and interpret. Francis Schaeffer, a Reformed theologian, wrote as part of the Berlin Congress on Evangelism 1966:

> Historic Christianity rests upon the truth of what today is called brute facts. Christ's redemptive and finished work actually took place at a point in space-time history within the universe. Historic Christianity rests upon the truth of these things in absolute antithesis to their not being true.

Third, it is similar in that there is an interplay of experience and interpretation. The New Testament itself does not simply present the events of Jesus's life, it interprets. John 20:30 : "Now Jesus did many other signs in the presence of his disciples which are not written in this book, but these are written that you may believe that Jesus is the Christ, the Son of God." In theology there is an interplay of experience and interpretation, an interplay which is also echoed in science.

Fourth, the importance of community. We have seen it in science, we see it also in the New Testament, as for example in Paul's image of the Body. I come from a charismatic background in terms of Christian churchmanship. As you may know, in those circles there is always a debate about prophecy. How do you know that words given within the congregation are true? The New Testament, in dealing with the problem, talks about community. In I Corinthians 14 it says, "Let two or three prophets speak and let the others weigh what is said". The importance of community in testing truth. If we had time we could further talk about common language, experience and tradition.

Fifth, the evaluation of truth. It proceeds often along similar lines to science. We ask questions about coherence, comprehensiveness, consistency.

Therefore, in view of all these facts I would want to argue that, in similarity with science, theology is a critical realist approach to the world. It involves an interplay of experience and interpretation. However, there are some differences, and we shall look at those now.

First, the degree of personal involvement. If we had more time, I would like to have done a third section on the social sciences. It seems to me that, if physical sciences have personal involvement, the social sciences have even greater personal involvement in the act of knowing, and theology probably has greater still. So there is a continuum, an increasing amount of personal involvement in the act of knowing in those three areas of study. Indeed, in the Bible, 'knowing' is all about that in which I am personally involved. In John 8: 31 Jesus says, "If you continue in my word you will truly be my disciples and you will know the truth and the truth will set you free". We talk about faith, trust, confidence. These are relationship words in terms of experiencing and knowing truth. There is an American Quaker called Parker Palmer, one of whose books is entitled 'To Know as We are Known: The Spirituality of Education' [Harper & Rowe (1983)]. In it he argues that to know is to be known. There is both the active part of knowing and the passive part of knowing. It is like letting knowledge go through you, exposing your ideas. We say that in terms of our relationship with God, in terms of the way in which we need also to be passive in the act of knowing. We did not love God first, but he loved us.

Second, one has to say there is a slightly different subject matter, that is a personal infinite God rather than an impersonal universe. The nature of relationship changes one's method experimentally. As a physicist, if I want to test a hypothesis, I think of a controlled environment and of limited outcomes, and I rigorously test it. I don't think that, if I asked my wife whether she loves me, such a rigorous testing would be appreciated. The nature of relationship changes how one explores the reality. David Jenkins wrote:

> "God is no object of critical investigation. He is the object of faith and hope, of obedience, of love, of longing".

An infinite God, of course, means that we are always limited in our power to comprehend.

Third, it seems that there is no parallel in science to historical revelation which we find within theology, those particular events which have particular significance, focused for the Christian in the incarnation. As Paul wrote, "In Christ in whom we all find treasures of wisdom and knowledge" (Colossians 2:3).

Finally, there are different primary ways of describing the same reality. The primary interest of science is 'how' questions; the primary interest of theology is 'why' questions.

How do we think we know what we know in theology? We can say:

> By the subtle interplay of experience and interpretation, involving personal judgements within a committed community, and exploring and being explored by an objective personal reality.

So what I conclude is that, far from the popular image of the ways of knowledge in science and theology being very different indeed, there is considerable overlap. They are not entirely the same, but there are many similarities.

Conclusion

By now you might be rewriting the question to, "How does he know what he thinks he knows?"! I ask myself that. It seems to me that in trying to understand the nature of science, not just from a philosophical point of view but from the very history and experience of what it means to be a scientist, and then exploring a little of what theology is about, we see that there are similarities. And that, of course, is what this consultation is about and is what we shall be doing in the next couple of days. These ways of exploring the world have much in common, and yet have some differences. They pose questions about the whole human experience of reality. I think the basis for that is located in God himself. How do we know what we think we know under God? If we take seriously God's relationship with the universe, it warns us to be humble. There is an infinite omniscient deity whose thoughts are greater than ours, and we as creatures cannot reasonably expect to be like God in knowledge. We do have a finiteness and a fallenness which means that there will always be mystery and always more to explore. The dogmatism of either science's or theology's masterminds eventually reaches its limits. And yet with humility should also go hope, because this God of the universe is fundamentally a self-revealing God, a God who allows the universe order and our minds intelligence with which to explore it, a God who reveals himself in particular events as a God of love and grace. John 1:18 seems to sum up much of what I have attempted to say:

> "No one has ever seen God; but the only Son .... he has made him known".

So there is hope that we can know what we think we know.

QUESTIONS following Dr. Wilkinson's Lecture

Q. **Do you feel the question which is the title of your lecture can really be answered adequately solely from a Christian perspective without, taking account of the other religions in the world?**

A. I limited what I said partly because of the time available. Yet you raise an important point. I don't think Christian theology in its broadest sense cuts off other religious insights, though perhaps it has done so at various times in the past.

There is an increasing openness in addressing such questions, and certainly the question of pluralism in terms of this whole area of knowledge is a very important one. How do we know what is true if different people are saying different things about the same thing? Are they complementary truths or are they conflicting?

I can't deal with that whole question here and now, but I note the force of it. Perhaps it needs to be picked upon another occasion.

Q. **Do you not think that science explores objectively, but uses its discoveries subjectively?**

A. Science explores an objective reality, not just in an objective way, but involving subjective factors. Arthur Holmes, an American philosopher, wrote, "In all our objectivity there is subjectivity, and in all our subjectivity there is objectivity". That is not to say that despair of improving the quality of objective reality.

What you then do with the knowledge is an extremely important area. Something else for the agenda on another occasion!

Q. **I feel there are fewer differences between theology and science than you suggest. Do you not agree that revelation is also part of science?**

A. It depends what you mean by revelation. I agree that any true knowledge of the universe is inspired. I accept that the self-revealing nature of God is not found just in the particular events that we would call'Gospel', but that the logos underlies the whole creation. Where truth is truth, that is about the self-revealing God allowing human minds to grasp and to understand and to know.

The only differences I would insist upon would be particular events which disclose the nature of the God of the Bible as the God of love and grace and action within the universe.

Q. **You have spoken of 'finiteness' and a 'fallenness' in reference to the human situation. Do you equate those two?**

A. I don't equate them. I think our finiteness is not just a sign of our moral fallenness. It is a fact that we are creatures in face of a creator.

I think, however, there is something about the human nature which means that our ability to understand and discern the world has been corrupted or perverted by not being in the right relationship with the creator. Not totally or irrevocably. I wouldn't want to argue that a person who is an atheist has no ability to do science. But in the whole enterprise of discerning knowledge there is something which limits us by our incorrect use of minds and resources in our exploring of the world.

2. By [illegible] what [illegible] by revelation, I accept the [illegible] [illegible] of the [illegible] [illegible]. I accept that the self-[illegible] [illegible] God is [illegible] in the particular [illegible] [illegible] [illegible] [illegible] [illegible] [illegible] [illegible] [illegible] [illegible] [illegible] [illegible] [illegible] [illegible] [illegible] [illegible] [illegible] [illegible].

The [illegible] [illegible] I would [illegible] [illegible] would be [illegible] [illegible] that [illegible] the [illegible] [illegible] of the [illegible] the God of love and [illegible] [illegible] within the universe.

[illegible]

A: I do not equate them. I think our uniqueness is not a sign of our moral goodness. It is a fact that we are [illegible] in [illegible] [illegible] [illegible].

I think, however, there is something about the human nature which means that our ability to understand and [illegible] the world [illegible] been [illegible] or [illegible] by [illegible] [illegible] [illegible] [illegible] [illegible]. Not [illegible] of the world.

Mind and Brain

Dr. John Sloper

One of our previous speakers discussed at some length the philosophical question "How do I know what I think I know?" Within the medical profession we have our own approaches to knowledge which differ in different branches of the profession. A physician is said to be someone who knows everything, but does nothing for his patients, whereas a surgeon is someone who knows nothing, but does everything; a psychiatrist is someone who knows nothing and does nothing; and, with apologies to Professor Garner, a pathologist is someone who knows everything and does everything - but it's too late to do the patient any good. And, although not entirely serious, these definitions contain a considerable element of truth. As a surgeon I have to work in a very practical world. I have to make decisions based on our present knowledge of the body and act on them. Essentially I know whether I'm right or not by what Mrs Jones comes back and tells me next week. She will either come back very pleased and say "I can see now, doctor" or she will tell me very politely that I was wrong by saying something like "It hasn't really helped me very much, doctor". In general, medicine is more directly related to observation than, for example, theoretical physics. We do build our castles in the air, but they are much more modest and we know fairly quickly whether they are going to fall down.

My talk will be divided into three main parts.

First, I will describe something of our present understanding of the structure and function of the brain, both at the microscopic level and at an organisational level, to give an idea of the huge complexity of the mechanisms involved and of how little we really understand. I will then move on to describe more clinically related observations about the interdependence of brain structure and function. Finally, I will try and relate these observations to our ideas of mind and what it means to be human.

Essentially the brain consists of a collection of nerve cells. In the simplest animals, for example cockroaches, a relatively small number of nerve cells are connected together in ways that can be worked out. The human brain uses similar neurons as its basic building blocks, but in very much larger numbers. The structure of an individual nerve cell can be studied under the microscope by precipitating a particular combination of chemicals inside it to outline it. It has recently become possible to place the tip of a microelectrode inside a single nerve cell and record its electrical activity, then to inject a dye into the cell and study the same cell under the light or electron microscope. For an individual nerve cell it is possible to study its activity, determine what it responded to in the brain and then study its structure and connections. A typical nerve cell is rather like a tree with a bulbous trunk and a single, very long fine root that branches and spreads out a long way from the trunk. The bulbous part of the trunk is the cell body which contains the nucleus and the major metabolic machinery of the cell. A typical nerve cell body is about 20 microns in diameter, about a fiftieth of a millimetre. The equivalents of the branches of the tree are called dendrites and are the major receiving surface of the neuron. The equivalent of the root system is called the axon and transmits impulses from the neuron to the dendrites of other neurons. A typical neuron would receive maybe 10,000 contacts, called synapses, from the axons of other neurons and its axon would make a similar number of synapses with the dendrites of other neurons. Electrical signals from many sources arrive at the dendrites of a single neuron, the inputs are processed by the neuron and an output is generated which passes as impulses down its axon to activate other neurons.

I am now going to increase the magnification and look at some of these things more closely. The dendrites of many neurons have little side branches, rather like the leaves on our tree, only shaped like miniature mushrooms. These are called dendritic spines. Under the electron microscope an individual spine has a stalk and a head which is connected by a structure called a synapse to a terminal from the axon of another nerve cell. This axon terminal contains little bubble-like structures called vesicles which contain the chemical transmitter used by that cell. When electrical impulses travel down the axon to one of its terminals, those transmitter bubbles are released and open 'gates' into the spine. These allow ions to enter the dendrite through the spine and so an electric current flows into the neuron and activates it. Other axon terminals make synapses directly with the dendrite or cell body of the neuron. In general synapses on to spines excite the neuron while those on to the cell body inhibit its activity.

To move to a still smaller scale, pictures have recently been published of the structure of the individual molecules that form the ionic gates described above. They are shaped rather like an elongated doughnut, this structure being determined by the molecular biological mechanisms that Professor Miller described earlier. These molecules roll themselves up into a tube. The tube changes shape when the transmitter molecule attaches to it and this enlarges the central hole to allow ions to pass through. So we know a lot about the structure and function of neurons and of mechanisms by which they communicate with each other. In particular the role of chemicals in synaptic transmission is important. Different neuronal types and pathways use their own particular transmitter. Drugs are available which can either increase or reduce the effect of individual transmitters and so selectively influence the activity of particular parts of the brain and affect behaviour.

I am now going to move a long way back up the scale of magnification. Most of what we see when viewing the human brain is a folded sheet of grey matter called the cerebral cortex. If unfolded this would cover about two square feet and varies from about two to five millimetres in thickness. This sheet is made up of millions and millions of nerve cells; in fact no really reliable estimates of total numbers of neurons in the human brain have been made. Within the cortex the neuronal cell bodies are embedded in a complex tangle of axons and dendrites which interconnect them. Some of these connections are short and some form bundles of axons which run together to or from distant brain regions. Deep to the cortex lie other groups of neurons which serve different functions and which also receive and send connections to other parts of the brain and spinal cord. The essential working hypothesis of neuroscientists is that all brain functions depend on the activity and interconnections of these many different groups of nerve cells. I would emphasise that this is only a working hypothesis, but as yet I know of no evidence of any brain function that has been shown to be independent of the activity of nerve cells.

What I want to do now is to talk a bit more about the overall organisation of the brain. At the very simplest level the nervous system has a sensory input, whether it comes from touch on the skin or through images entering the eyes or sound reaching the ears. This input is received and translated into nerve impulses which go along the sensory nerves. The axons in these nerves will activate nerve cells in the spinal cord that are connected directly to a muscle and produce a movement. If I were to tap your knee tendon your leg would jerk. That is a simple and predictable reflex and is the simplest type of link between input and output. In very simple terms what happens in more complex reactions is that much more processing is interposed between the input and response. The incoming signal is analysed in more detail, it may be compared to memories and other activity can act upon it before a more complex output is produced. The brain has been regarded as a series of increasingly more complex loops interposed between input and output. For example, when you have a conversation with someone, you hear their words which are being carried into your brain from your ears, you recognise and understand what is being said, you consider your answer and then you activate your motor pathways to make a reply.

A great deal is now known about the pathways involved in both sensory transmission and motor functions. For example there are sensory receptors in the skin which are specifically sensitive to heat and send impulses along sensory nerves when stimulated. The brain knows that these signals represent heat because it knows that these nerves come from heat receptors, not because of the pattern of nerve impulses carried. The impulse rate codes for the temperature of the stimulus, being faster if the stimulus is hotter. The impulses pass along particular temperature pathways in the spinal cord where they make local connections, but also continue upwards to the cerebral cortex. If the stimulus is hot enough to be damaging, the local reflex connections cause muscle contractions which withdraw the limb being burnt to prevent further damage. This often occurs before the signals reach the cortex and before you become aware that you are being burnt. This illustrates for a particular pathway the presence of parallel low level and high level loops. There are a number of different sensory pathways and different subdivisions within them. The nerves from the eyes give a different type of sensation from nerves from the skin and a light touch activates a different pathway from heat or pain.There are also several different pathways from areas of the brain controlling movement which converge on the cells in the spinal cord that send axons out to the muscles. Between these inputs and outputs there are a huge number of possible interconnections.

So there are specific anatomical pathways to and from the brain which perform different functions and in a similar way different parts within the brain itself perform different roles. Certain areas of the brain are involved in basic survival functions, such as breathing and control of blood pressure. At higher levels other parts are involved with things like appetite and sexual drive. In the cerebral cortex are higher level functions, with different parts of the cortex dealing with different types of activity. We know this because, in animal experiments, certain localised brain areas have been removed surgically and certain functions have been found to be lost and because patients who have had strokes affecting particular brain areas have specific disabilities. For example, one area of the cortex receives the input from the eyes. If part of that area is damaged the patient will lose vision in a localised part of their field of vision. Other cortical areas are concerned with touch and hearing; together these areas are termed the primary sensory areas. Similarly there is a primary motor area which is involved in the control of movement. The function of these areas has been especially studied and is reasonably well understood. More complex processing occurs through connections from these to other cortical areas known as association areas. Most of the work on these areas has been done in relation to vision. Recent work has shown that processing of colour is separated from the recognition of objects and the detection of movement. The visual areas of the brain are like a committee, with different areas doing different jobs. In general terms the recognition of objects is processed separately from spatial relationships. So one part of the brain recognises a post box, another part tells you that it is standing outside a Post Office and a third part tells you that it is red. How these separate processing pathways recombine their information to give an integrated picture is not understood.

I have already said a little about how nerve cells function. Scientists have recorded activity from individual neurons in the different visual areas of the cortex. By putting an electrode very close to, or inside, an individual neuron its activity can be recorded when the eyes are stimulated by patterns of light and so we can study what excites that particular cell. In the primary visual cortex nerve cells respond to a light or dark edge, but, for a specific cell, that edge has to be at a particular orientation. Cells that recognise a particular orientation are grouped together in clusters. So at this cortical level there are mechanisms for recognising edges and their orientations. In subsequent cortical areas are neurons that respond to more complex stimulus features, such as the distance of an object, and after further processing cells are found which respond to complex stimuli such as faces.

The localisation of different functions in different parts of the brain applies at least in part to some higher level brain functions. Different aspects of language are localised to different areas which are only found on one side of the brain. Many people will be familiar with the tragic consequences of some strokes when patients are left unable to speak. They are still able to hear and understand but they can't express what they want to say. Some of them recover and they will tell you how frustrating it was. I saw a patient a little while ago who had a recent onset of difficulty in reading. She could see the letters but they no longer made sense to her. She could no longer recognise the patterns of letters that made up words because of a problem in a particular part of the visual association cortex. I have also seen a similar problem where a patient could hear words but not understand their meaning. So these more complex levels of processing also depend on specific brain areas.

In general we know a lot about individual nerve cells and their structure, function and responses, but we know much less about how they work together in groups. To give an idea of the scale of the problem, a hard working colleague of mine spent three years doing electron microscopy. At the end of this time he estimated that he had examined about half a cubic millimetre of brain. Other people have spent several years reconstructing an individual neuron using electron microscope sections. Although we can get very detailed information about individual cells it takes a long time. The number of individual cells studied by being injected with dye after having their activity recorded probably still only runs into hundreds compared to the many millions of cells in a mammalian brain.

What I have discussed so far has been brain function at a fairly low level. But what about the mind? Is there any difference between brain function and mind? What evidence is there that such things as memory, intellect, personality, mood and volition depend on the structure and function of the brain? Before approaching this question I want to come back to a slightly simpler level and discuss evidence of how sensory perception depends on brain structure and function. I talked earlier about pain pathways. I am sure that you have had the experience of putting you foot into a bath which is too hot and pulling it out quickly. When you put your foot into the hot water you experience an immediate sharp pain. After you have pulled it out you experience a later wave of dull pain. The reason for this is that there are two different pathways conducting pain sensation from the foot and impulses in one of these travel along the nerves much faster than in the other. Both sets of pain signals start off from your foot at the same time, but those in the slowly conducting pathway take longer to reach the brain. So you are actually perceiving the same event twice because of the structure and transmission properties of the pathways involved. The same is true to a lesser extent of the visual pathways. There are also fast and slowly conducting visual axons. The effect is not as easily demonstrated but signals about movement and the colour of objects arrive at slightly different times. These observations raise interesting questions about our perception of time and simultaneity The definition of 'now' as the instant between past and present poses a number of problems. I suspect that in terms of brain function 'now' is not instantaneous but is a finite length of time and that sensory experience is integrated over this period.

Another example of the sensory apparatus determining what we see occurs after removal of a cataract. The patient will often come back and say that everything appears much more blue. In part this is because many cataracts are yellow and absorb blue light, but it is also because the normal lens absorbs ultra-violet light, even though the retina is sensitive to it. Following removal of the cataract, the patient can now see ultraviolet light that they could not see previously.

Many optical illusions depend on the way the brain processes visual information. The brain makes assumptions about the relative sizes of objects and, if these relative sizes are changed, objects can be made to appear nearer or further away. Perception is also changed by learning and experience. When I first started electron microscopy, the structures I saw were unrecognisable. After a few weeks I found that I was seeing things that I couldn't see previously. Similarly musicians learn to hear particular aspects of music, for example learning to follow a bass part or pick out a particular instrument when listening to a piece of music. We only perceive what our senses allow us to perceive, but we can change this to some extent by training and experience.

To return to the aspects of mind that I described earlier, what evidence is there that memory, intellect, personality, mood and volition depend on, and are influenced by, brain structure and activity? These functions are more difficult to localise than the sensory and motor functions described above, in part at least because we know much less about them. Nevertheless there is abundant evidence that they depend on the structural integrity of the brain and are influenced by things that affect its function.

Memories are probably recorded in widespread brain areas, but an area called the hippocampus, found on each side at the base of the brain, is known to be very important for the laying down of new memories. One patient has been described who unfortunately had to have these areas removed and lost the ability to lay down new memories. His memory span became seconds, he lived for the instant and had no recollection of what had happened previously. It is a common experience that, as a result of brain changes that occur with age, some people have difficulty remembering recent events although they can recall events from the distant past in great detail. Head injuries disrupt the processes involved in the laying down of memories of recent events so that we actually assess the severity of a head injury in part by how much the patient can remember from before the blow. Can they remember hitting their head? Can they remember up to ten minutes before the injury or can they only remember things from the previous day? The longer the memory has been laid down, the more resistant it is to mechanical disruption. Fleeting glimpses of recalled memories have also been produced by electrical stimulation of the cortex of conscious patients during brain surgery for epilepsy. So there is plenty of evidence that memory depends on the integrity of brain function, with hints that specific memories may be held in particular locations.

Intellect is difficult to define precisely, but is fairly well understood as an aspect of brain function. Many people will be familiar with the tragic results of Alzheimer's disease, pre-senile dementia, in which intellectual function is slowly but inexorably lost. This disease has a physical basis which is slowly being unravelled. Nerve cells in the cortex of patients with Alzheimer's disease contain an abnormal protein, which gives a very characteristic appearance under the microscope, and there is a loss of nerve cells and their connections. So intellect depends on the integrity of brain structure, particularly in what are termed higher centres such as the cerebral cortex.

Changes in personality can also be caused by damage to parts of the brain. One well-described example is that of a man who had both the frontal lobes of his cortex destroyed in an accident during the building of the American railways at the end of the last century. From being a responsible family man he became completely irresponsible and almost childlike. It is not unusual for patients to become difficult and aggressive after serious head injuries and to be described by their relatives as having become completely different people. Changes in personality were also seen after the operation of frontal leucotomy which was performed for very severe depression. The results of this operation were controversial because of the major changes in personality produced, but it did allow some people to live outside an institution when they previously had no meaningful existence because of overwhelming anxieties and obsessions. The effects on personality in one patient were described as having changed him from being a totally neurotic professor to a happy roadsweeper. Whether this was to his advantage is debatable, but brain surgery or injury can undoubtedly produce major personality changes.

Mood also depends on brain function. Depression responds to particular types of drugs and other drugs produce depression as a side effect. Severe depressive episodes are undoubtedly shortened by electro-convulsive therapy (ECT). This is probably rather like mending a watch by hitting it with a hammer, but nevertheless it works. And many of the drugs of abuse are addictive because of the effects that they have in lifting mood and producing feelings of euphoria. Feelings of pleasure can also be produced by electrical stimulation of certain very localised areas of the brain. This has been inferred from animal experiments in which electrodes have been implanted in certain brain areas and the animal has been given a pedal by which it can produce stimulation of that area. In these experiments a rat will repeatedly press the pedal, even in preference to eating and drinking, and it is presumed that this is because the stimulation produces a pleasurable feeling. Similar findings have been made in patients where electrodes implanted in similar areas have been used to treat intractable pain in terminally ill patients. These brain areas contains endorphins, peptide transmitters which have a similar structure to morphine, and it is thought that it is this similarity which makes morphine and other opiates addictive.

What about volition and the ability to do what you want to do? In

Parkinson's disease the characteristic deficit is the disconnection of the patients' volition from their ability to carry out their intention. They know what they want to do but are unable to do it. For example they cannot make their foot move in spite of making tremendous mental efforts to produce the physical movement. The link between volition and action has been broken by the disease process which involves the degeneration of a particular brain pathway that uses dopamine as a transmitter. This transmitter can be replaced at least in part by a synthetic drug called L-DOPA which is now widely used to treat Parkinson's disease. When L-DOPA was first introduced its effects were graphically described by the neurologist Oliver Sachs who recorded his patients' experiences in a book called 'Awakenings'. Suddenly the patients could move again, they could talk and they could express their frustration at having been locked inside their brains unable to do what they wanted. So although we cannot identify a part of the brain which contains the will, we can define at least one pathway through which it acts.

Finally what about consciousness? As scientists we cannot define consciousness, but we do know that it depends on the integrity of brain structure. Certain areas of the brainstem which have very widespread connections to higher centres are essential for the maintenance of consciousness. If these areas are destroyed the brain becomes permanently unconscious. This doesn't mean, of course, that consciousness resides in these areas, but simply that they are essential for maintaining consciousness. In a similar way the switch on a television is essential to make it work, but does not itself produce the picture.

In the lecture so far I have presented evidence that those things we call "mind" depend on the structure and function of the brain in the same way as the analysis of sensory information and the control of movement do. But there is also evidence that the opposite is true, that the structure and function of the brain depend on its activity and can be modified by it. The best worked out example of this is the development of the visual system. If a child cannot use one eye, for example, because an eyelid droops in front of it for a period of time when the child is small, then the vision in that eye will be impaired. The eye is said to become amblyopic and if the condition is not treated the reduction in vision will be permanent. Animal experiments have shown that this reduction in vision is accompanied by changes in the structure and function of visual parts of the brain. Nerve cells connected to the eye that is covered become smaller, those connected to the normal eye become larger and the responses of cells in the visual cortex become dominated by the uncovered eye at the expense of the covered eye. So simply because one eye has not been used for a time, the brain changes markedly in both structure and function. This only happens during a period of sensitivity early in life, up to about seven years of age, but shows very clearly that changing the input to the brain can have profound effects on it.

In simple animals, patterns of electrical activity in nerve cells have been shown to modify the strength of connections between them, and this is regarded as a model of simple learning. Evidence has been produced for similar mechanisms in higher animals and there seems little doubt that electrical and biochemical changes of some sort underlie learning processes in man. This implies that mental processes involved in learning are changing the structure of the brain and its connections. The brain processes underlying learning and intelligence are also to some extent under genetic control. To what extent this is so has been a subject of great controversy, and there are undoubtedly major environmental influences at work as well, but at the very least there are a number of genetic disorders such as Down's syndrome in which intelligence and the ability to learn are severely impaired.

The idea for which I have presented evidence above is essentially that mind is a manifestation of brain function and not separate from it. This would be accepted as a working hypothesis by most neuroscientists and has been termed mind-brain identity. Our experience, thoughts and feelings depend on brain function and the brain in turn is influenced by our mental activity. I don't think that this in anyway devalues human experience any more than a piece of music is devalued because it is played on a length of stretched, dried intestine from a cow. The fact that we exist and experience life through a physical mechanism does not devalue us. But this now raises the major problem - what do I mean by 'we'. Everything I have talked about so far as a scientist has been from the outside of the brain looking in. But I don't exist like that. I'm on the inside looking out. And, although I can't prove it, I work on the assumption that you all exist in the same way. This is the central mystery of existence. It is not really mind in the sense that we have been using the term because such things as intelligence and emotion can be observed from the outside. Nothing that I have talked about solves the basic problem of what 'I' am inside my brain.

When a person dies, their brain ceases to function and the 'I' ceases to exist in any form that we can recognise directly. Is there any aspect of brain structure or function that can continue to exist independently of the brain? As a scientist I can't answer that question. Electrical activity of the brain ceases at death and the structure of the brain disintegrates fairly rapidly. All I can say is that patterns can exist independently of the elements that make them up. Perhaps the best known example of this is a computer program. It can exist in the memory of one computer. It can be translated into an entirely different form on a floppy disc and can then be recreated in the memory of a different computer.

The program is an abstract pattern that can exist in many different physical forms. The brain has an abstract pattern that can potentially exist in other forms. At a very simple level that pattern is what anatomy textbooks contain. If you were to do a Spock and be dematerialised, has the molecular pattern of your body transmitted elsewhere and the body and brain recreated, would you be the same? That isn't a question that I or any other scientist can answer.

Finally, is there anything about the human brain which makes us unique and separates us from other animals? The human brain is bigger than that of most animals, but not bigger than the brains of many of the whale family. It is the biggest of the primate brains, but it has not been shown to be essentially different. The sheet of cortex in man is larger than in other primates, but appears to have enlarged by adding more of the same cortical modules rather than by adding anything distinctively new. In many ways this is analogous to plugging more memory into a computer. On the other hand I have recently replaced my ancient computer with one with more memory. The memory in the new one is essentially the same as in the old, but because of the increased capacity the computer can run much more complex programs and appears to have a totally different personality. There are many striking similarities in both the structure and function of neurons between different species, including man, and there are many similarities in the organisation of brain pathways and areas, at least for the lower levels of sensory analysis. However the human brain continues a trend present throughout the mammals by having a great increase in the size of the cortical association areas, where many of the higher level functions, including language, are found. So having much more cortex may allow the human brain to undertake more complex and new types of function, as with my new computer. Our methods of examining the human remain very limited. A neuropathologist examined Einstein's brain and found nothing remarkable. It is quite possible that more differences will be found between human and animal brains, but our present picture is that of a brain that is at the top end of the spectrum of primate evolution - and to use the word top may be simply a reflection of human vanity.

I learnt my approach to scientific method from my first physics teacher at grammar school. He got us to open a double page of our exercise book and write out a general experimental plan. In the top left we wrote 'What we did'; in the bottom left 'How we did it'; in the top right we wrote 'What we found'; and in the bottom right 'So what?' I have described at considerable length the 'What we found' of neuroscience but it is really the 'So what' that is most important. I have talked about mind/brain identity and I think that there is little doubt that mental function depends on the physical existence of the brain. We are constrained by our brains in terms of perception and action, since destroying bits of brain prevents us from doing certain things. I've talked a little about the nature versus nurture problems with intelligence and I hope that I have shown that we have enormous influence over our brains. One of the reasons I went back into clinical medicine from neuroscience research was the human spirit. I enjoy working with patients. I admire patients who battle with great visual difficulties. I admire the elderly couple who come into the clinic; the wife can't see and her husband brings her in gently by the hand. Faith is likewise a valuable thing. And I don't think any of this is in any way devalued by saying that it occurs in a physical structure, that being human depends on the human brain. Scientists and philosophers have great difficulty defining what it means to be human looking from the outside. For example, behavioural scientists talk in terms of the use of language and tools, but other species communicate by sound and chimpanzees make and use tools. What it is to be human is something that I can only define from the inside of my brain looking out.

QUESTIONS following Dr Sloper's lecture:

Q. **Is there any truth in the correlation between aluminium and Alzheimer's disease?**

A. Some evidence has been produced to suggest a link but it is not proved. Differences in aluminium levels in drinking water in different areas around Newcastle have been correlated with differences in the incidence of Alzheimer's disease and aluminium toxicity has been shown to produce a rather different form of dementia in a few patients on renal dialysis. Animal fed with aluminium have produced appearances in their brains which have some similarities with those in patients with Alzheimer's disease. But there are also other abnormalities in Alzheimer's disease and any link with aluminium is still controversial.

Q. **How important is the relative timing with which signals reach all those different synapses?**

A. In some instances it is very important. There are nerve cells in the brainstem which receive inputs from both ears. These localise sounds in space by the difference in time at which sounds from the two ears reach them. I'm sure timing is important in other types of analyses, but how precise it needs to be and how it affects them I don't know.

Q. **What can we do to enhance memory recall?**

A. Practice obviously plays a big part and there are well recognised techniques of memorising by association. Certain drugs have been claimed to help memory in Alzheimer's disease by stimulating specific cholinergic pathways but these claims are strongly disputed.

Q. **Why is it that in our personalities we differ so? Some people are cold, some warm, some only very intellectual, some very emotional. In the context of Christian commitment, I've long considered that, unless the emotion is stirred somewhere along the line, Christian commitment will be imperfect.**

A. There are areas of the brain called the limbic system which appear to be involved in emotional responses, but I suspect that emotion may also be a more general aspect of brain function. I'm sure that there is a genetic component to personality and that personality traits are to some extent inherited but they are also to a considerable extent learnt. The relative importance of the inherited and learnt components is very difficult to determine.

Q. **Are there characteristics of the female brain which are different from the male brain?**

A. An eminent anatomist once said that anatomy tells you nothing about function, but that nothing is definite. The female brain is definitely smaller on average than the male brain. It doesn't mean that it doesn't work as well, nor that it works differently. As a matter of experience there are some things that women are better at than men and vice versa. To what extent these differences are genetically determined, and to what extent they are learnt, is controversial.

Q. **Is it sensible to suggest that the human brain is able to produce what in religious language we call visions?**

A. Undoubtedly the brain can produce visions. Schizophrenia, for example, is characterised by hallucinations. The patients may hear voices and some see things. Patients who lose the sight in one eye can be quite disturbed by the visions they see until you explain to them that it is quite normal for the brain to make up images, compensating for what the eye can no longer see. The brain is very good at making assumptions about what ought to be there. There are classes of drugs called hallucinogens, like LSD, which will produce very vivid visual sensations. What this implies for religious visions and whether they are something different is not a question that I can answer as a scientist. All we can say is that there are brain mechanisms which can produce visions.

Q. **Could you comment on what is happening in the brain when one is asleep and dreaming?**

A. There are two kinds of sleep. There is the so-called deep sleep and there is rapid eye movement sleep. During the rapid eye movement sleep the brain is much more active. Quite what is happening in terms of brain function is not really known. There are lots of theories, such as that you are reorganising memories of the events of the past day. No one even knows why we need sleep, or how much sleep we need, except that if you deprive people of sleep for too long they stop functioning properly and their efficiency drops. No one knows either what the dreaming component of sleep is. But it seems to be essential because after sleep deprivation the dreaming sleep is made up more than the non-dreaming sleep. Dreams often appear to be related to what has been happening in everyday life. Animals appear to dream as well because they show the same external signs of dreaming as humans do.

Q. **Have we found any evidence for extra-sensory perception?**

A. The brain generates electrical waves that can be recorded from the surface of the scalp, and presumably there is a very weak electrical field around the brain. Having said that, I know of no convincing evidence that any form of extra-sensory perception has been demonstrated to the satisfaction of the general scientific community. The basic problem is that many of the lay people interested in this subject don't understand statistics. If you do an experiment twenty times you will on average get one statistically significant result purely on a random basis.

Q. **Some recent work on the brain has included the detection of very low magnetic fields in the brain. This enables us to localise areas of activity in the brain during certain types of behaviour. You can say that this is extra-sensory perception in the sense that there is external perception of activity going on in the brain. The next step is then to get that into another brain. At the moment that is done through hardware. An interesting point was made in a 'Horizon' programme on television last week. All we can see in testing through hardware is flashes of light. However, if you ask somebody a question and they want to say 'yes', light flashes in one place; if they want to say 'no', it flashes somewhere else. So without a person actually having to articulate the answer, you could know what they were thinking simply by watching where the flash comes. So isn't that a picture of extra-sensory perception?**

A. Not in the sense that I would understand it. It is another way of observing from the outside what is going on in the brain, but I don't see any difference in principle between that and recording nerve cell activity using a microelectrode to find what activates it. It is powerful evidence of the localisation of higher brain functions that I was talking about earlier, but I can often tell whether someone is going to say 'yes' or 'no' by the expression on their face. The problem is getting information into the other person's brain by bypassing their sensory pathways. That is the essential element that has not been demonstrated.

Q. **Have you any comments on the generalisation that the brain's left hemisphere deals with organisation, logic, control and maleness,**

and the right deals with intuition, shapes, holism and femaleness?

A. One of the themes of this lecture has been that many functions, including what we term higher functions, are localised to specific brain areas. There is no doubt that there are differences in function between the left and right hemispheres. The most obvious example is language that I talked about earlier but there are others. The problem is how to categorise the kind of activities that you described without making gross oversimplifications. There are many differences between individuals. For example there are artists and scientists, visual mathematicians who do geometry and abstract mathematicians who work with equations. Different people think in different ways that are presumably related to different patterns of brain function.

Q. **We have body transplants. We might even become able to breed pigs to provide hearts for humans. How much do you think transplants could take place in the head?**

A. First there is a philosophical problem. I don't think there is such a thing as a whole brain transplant. Since your brain is what defines you most, it is arguable that it would be a case of transplanting a new body onto the brain rather than the other way round. That then is really no different from putting in a new heart, only more so. The major problem with the brain is that it does not heal. The central nervous system does not repair itself in the sense of restoring full function. So even if you could technically move the brain to a new body it would not remake its connections. What has been done is to transplant small groups of neuronal cells, particularly as part of the research into the treatment of Parkinson's disease. Results in man have been disappointing so far although some animal work has been more successful. During infancy a lot of brain development seems to depend on experience. A lot of extra connections are made by nerve cells during development and then those that are not used wither away leaving the most used connections. A lot of experience has gone into building the connections in an adult brain. How these could be rebuilt in transplanted nervous tissue poses a major challenge.

Psychology: The Science of the Human Person

Professor David Booth

The focus of this year's Initiative is on the Life Sciences. Psychology, as a (or the) science of behaviour, fits in extremely well as a third life science alongside molecular biology and neuroscience. In fact, psychology has been a science of human life twice as long as biochemistry or genetics have been, and many times longer than the pinnacle of brain research, integrative neurophysiology. Moreover, all parts of psychology can be related to the biological sciences: the mind is built on our animal nature. Psychology is not a part of biology, though, in the narrower sense that zoology and physiology are. It cannot be, because we are also creatures of cultural history, educated into a society of talkers and thinkers.

Psychology on the intellectual map

Like all the sciences, a science of persons would presuppose that we are physical beings, made entirely of atoms. In other words, physics is taken to be the basic science. Nevertheless, the riposte to Rutherford's claim that the rest is stamp collecting must be that even the picture on a postage stamp is more than a mere collection of atoms. Indeed, psychologists and other scientists, including quite a few physicists these days, are not limited by Rutherford's lack of interest in the mechanisms of colour perception and aesthetic appreciation!

As well as being physical, we are also social beings. Our life is shot through with language, to take a key example. Indeed, the conceptual analysis is perhaps the basic humanities discipline. Psychologists may seem rather philistine in their initial struggles to investigate beauty, happiness and love. Yet CERN does not laugh at Rutherford's atom-smashing efforts. The human mind is fearfully and wonderfully made. Decades of intensive experimental and observational research into language have now made psycholinguistics into a realistic, powerful and even sensitive subdiscipline. Psychologists are now introducing a tougher-minded openness to evidence into some of the subtler social science methods such as content analysis and qualitative research.

Hence, psychology is unique in being arguably both a natural science and a scientific humanities discipline. Psychology is in part a natural science. In that respect it is a life science, because it deals with the mentally organised behaviour of contemporary Homo sapiens and that of members of other animal species too, particularly mammals and birds (although ethologists, or behavioural zoologists, deal more widely with other species.)

Yet psychology (like ethology) is no less a social science as well. It is the systematic empirical study of the individual performing her or his role within the living cosmos of human society

On the other hand, some psychologists have argued fiercely that their discipline is either not a natural science or not like the social sciences. In my view, psychology has no reliable models in either biology or sociology, let alone in physics or economics. Psychology is the autonomous cognitive science of human behaviour. It must build its own paradigms, although there can be important insights into systems to be drawn from disciplines such as physiology, engineering, ecology and economics.

The whole person

The point is that, whatever way you draw the academic map, psychologists face a brutally simple but devastatingly complex empirical fact. This fact is that the human behaviour that is the primary object of their study is comprised of the actions and reactions of a whole person.

First, the mental processes informing human behaviour are embodied. Indeed, they are based on the "wetware" engineering of neurophysiology: as Dr. Sloper said, there is no human mind without the human brain. Furthermore, as Professor Miller implied, the cells and their arrangement within any organ of the body, including the brain, mature in ways that depend on genetic programming, albeit in interaction with their developing surroundings within the organism and with its dynamic physical development.

Yet, secondly, the mind is also intrinsically social and, indeed, 'culturally' based. There is no human mind without a human upbringing as well. To reach our full personhood, we have to be educated into at least one cultural tradition and working language. This provides transmission mechanisms by which social traditions can reproduce themselves. This is a problem for Richard Dawkins' nutty effort to reduce all life to genes and so he invents 'nemes' to work the miracle of social memory for which his theory gives no account.

I am of course referring only to the sort of person whom we can investigate scientifically, a fellow human being. In that case, a person develops and lives as a 'psycho-bio-social' unity. In the everyday terms used in the title of a psychology textbook (published by Scientific American), we are Social Animals.

There is King James' English for this, of course: you and I are 'living souls, made out of clay and as helpmeets for each other', created in 'the image of the Elohim', the triune incarnate Word. A person is a soul (not "has a soul"), is her or his body (alive and mortal) and is a social being (a self only in relation to others).

It was grounding in this ancient Jewish concept of personhood, at the centre of the biblical doctrine of human nature, that eased me from chemistry into the life sciences and neurobiology, on my way into psychology and indeed also into so-called linguistic philosophy (from the later Wittgenstein). Furthermore, this vision of 'earthly souls in community' has kept me realistically balanced and eclectic; while my science has been embroiled in antimentalistic behaviourism, a sadly disembodied and nonsocial cognitive science, battles between biological psychology and social psychology, divorce between experiment and observation, and other vicissitudes of psychological research and practice.

Many inside and outside the discipline attribute these controversies to the youth of psychology or to a bogus claim to be science at all. Supposedly, we lack a 'paradigm'. I disagree. One person is so complex and multifaceted, let alone the brain and the society that constitute that person, that we cannot expect a homogeneity or rate of progress in psychology greater than that shown even by physics in all its aspects, let alone by biology or indeed the social sciences.

Here is one example (not particularly technical) of the relevance to psychology of a biblical view of humanity:

Deep within our post-renaissance culture and the more behaviourist wing of psychology is a mechanical view of behaviour as movements in response to stimulation, much as a billiard ball needs a prod from a cue before it will move. In contrast, Genesis teaches that the earthman (Adam) and the mother of all living (Eve) were (and of course still are) created as living souls. A key characteristic of Life is 'irritability' as Professor Miller termed it. In the most complex forms of life, this is manifest as spontaneous behaviour. It is of the nature of awake animals to behave -to act out beliefs and values and to react emotionally within situations as they are perceived.

Now Newton advanced from Aristotle in the physics of motion by realising that forces were not needed to sustain motion. A force was only needed to change motion, e.g. accelerate an object or counter acceleration from gravity or deceleration from friction. Similarly, an organismic or soulish view of behaviour is an advance on the extreme stimulus-response view once rather uncharacteristically taken by the American psychologist Neal Miller. He postulated that reinforcing stimulation is needed even to get any behaviour out: the animal would not move unless forced. Instead of this Aristotelian' paradigm, we should take a 'Newtonian' view of behaviour (or even an 'Einsteinian' one, if we allow for social relativisation). In other words, stimuli are not goads into action of reaction. Rather, they are guides, patterns of information conveyed by the senses that channel the animal's or person's selection among alternative actions or the elicitation of different reactions. The performance of behaviour is constitutive of animals, as momentum is constitutive of physical objects (including human bodies, as all too evident each day on the roads!) If it doesn't process information, it isn't an animal -it is as mindless or soulless as a tree or a mountain out of human view.

Soul and Spirit

The aim here therefore is to illustrate how scientific methods can be used to discover how human beings work as whole systems. I'll do that first by involving you in two tiny experiments that bring out some aspects of how we see and remember. Then I'll briefly discuss a couple of major scientific issues from a psychological viewpoint. I'll end with a summary sketch of uses of psychology to help people.

Just before starting that, though, let me declare myself a 'compatibilist': God knows the truth; conflicts of view are our problem. The Creator has provided us with many sources of information and inspiration. The Book of scriptural Revelation is complemented by the Book of Nature. In technical terms, I have the epistemological pluralism of a critical realist.

Thus, I believe that the human mind or soul is as open as the human body to empirical study in all its aspects, using suitably adapted versions of the general methods of science and history.

Of course, neither psychological science nor scientific historiography can investigate a person's status before God, any more than empirical findings by themselves can decide questions of value such as what is right to do, what is worthy of admiration or indeed what is an appropriate objective for psychotherapy.

Also, the science of mind, like physics or biology, can only think the Creator's mundane thoughts after Him in His general pattern of sustaining providence. Science cannot come to conclusions about events where the Creator may have acted self-consistently beyond what we can repeatedly observe evidence for within the natural order.

Experimental analysis of mental processes

Psychology has an advantage, a bit like astronomy or botany, that some interesting phenomena are readily accessible. Indeed, unlike telescopes or gene-sequencing equipment, we carry our minds around with us (for free, as the Americans say). Even some long-known and much-studied phenomena can take you to the frontier of the unknown about the mind, although of course it is no longer likely that one study of such a phenomenon could yield a major new discovery.

The Müller - Lyer illusion

The first little experiment is from my undergraduate Lab Book. It's a visual illusion, in allusion to John Sloper's topic: indeed, thinking about this effect will show up some connections between psychology and neuroscience while also illustrating the distinction between mind and brain.

This illusion is an effect of arrow shapes that was first investigated by 19th Century German psychologists called Müller and Lyer. Here is a line with outward-pointing arrowheads (acute angles) at each end:

another line is added from one end, with an inward-pointing arrowhead (obtuse angles) on its end:

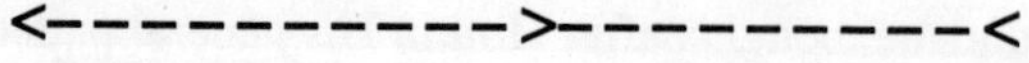

So now the two lines have a pair of arrowheads, one pair pointing in and the other pointing out. You might like to draw these two lines on separate pieces of card, making the line with the inward pointer longer than the line with the pair of acute angles on it (make the line continuous and the arrow flanges proportionately a bit longer than the the typed figure above); if you push the unarrowed end under the other card and arrange the two lines as above, you can adjust the length of the line going underneath so that it looks the same length as the line on top. I did this with an overhead projector at the meeting until about the same number of people said it should be shorter as said it should be longer. The two lines generally end up with the line between the acute angles shorter than the line between the obtuse angles, by about 10% on average. (If they look the same length above, count the hyphens and you'll find that strength of effect).

Why does the line with lines bent over it look shorter than a line with the same lines bent away from it? What is going on in our mind below the level of consciousness to give this illusory appearance? Why does the visual system work like this? This issue can be addressed in several ways. Even within science, there are different sorts of explanation.

In systems sciences like biology, ecology and psychology, there are 'functional' explanations, what Aristotle called 'final causation'. (They are teleological unless the system can be shown to have become that way as a result of the way it has operated). The usual immediate account given of the Müller-Lyer illusion is of this sort.

This idea is that size constancy creates the illusion. Size constancy results from visual angle (length on the retina) being used as a cue for distance. In some way, the visual system functions so that lines that are shorter on the retina because they are at a distance are seen as not so much shorter than nearer ones are seen: so to speak, the object is assumed to be of the same length even though it looks shorter further away.

For example, the retinal image, and indeed the artist's-eye-view, of railway tracks is of a distance between the rails as shorter as they get further away; yet the sleepers do not look shorter at the greater distance.

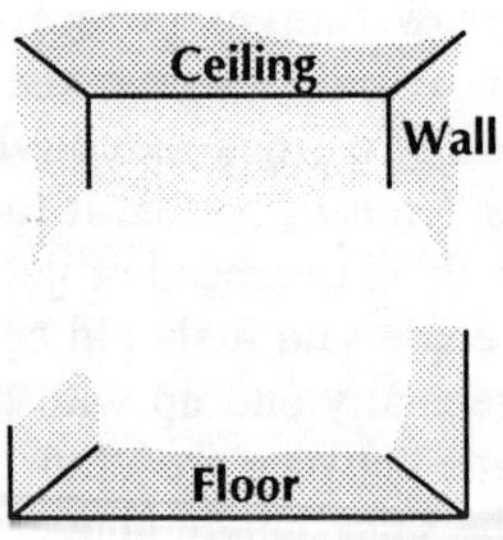

If you look from a doorway across a room at the line of the ceiling meeting the wall, the width of the wall looks the same as the width of the wall where you are standing as it abuts the floor; yet these two lines subtend very different angles in the field of view. Now the ceiling edge across the room has coming from each end the line of the corner between the walls and another line of the ceiling - wall junction: to draw this in perspective, these lines come off at obtuse angles, like an arrowhead pointing inwards (see diagram above). In contrast, the floor line near us has corners coming off it at acute angles.

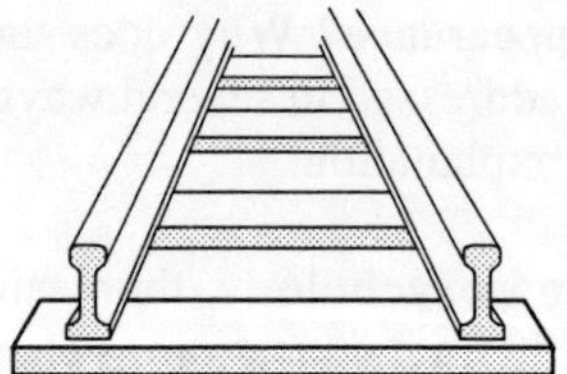

The same is at least half-true of the angles of the railway lines with distant and nearby sleepers (see diagram left). So the Müller-Lyer could be a part of how we need to see room structures, railways, roads, street and home furniture and so on.

Another sort of explanation of the illusion is 'ontogenic', invoking what I think Aristotle called 'original causation' or the conditions for development of the system. I believe that there is an old report that South African bushmen, who were used only to round huts, winding paths and straggly trees, are less subject to the illusion than people like us, brought up in societies with square-built houses, rectilinear crossroads and street furniture, etc.

Another ontogenetic theory would be that the genes program the visual system's connections for size constancy or whatever interactions between the lines in the diagram produced this illusion.

Genetic and environmental explanations of behaviour are often considered to be rivals. Geneticicists and psychologists will tell you about all sorts of muddle in this notion but suffice to say now that, in this case as probably most human and indeed mammalian behaviour, both explanations probably have part of the truth (as both previous speakers have said). Not directly relevant to this illusion but illustrating the general principle is the ontogeny of orientation sensitivity -the ability to tell the difference between angles off the vertical, for instance. (Dr. Sloper used this example in his discussion of "lazy eye"). Orientation-specific pathways in the visual system are initially connected up genetically but connections only persist if they are stimulated by visual input: thus, kittens reared in a world of vertical stripes bump into horizontal rods but not into vertical ones.

The molecular biologist Edelman has argued that you can account for all acquired structuring of the genetically indeterminate connectivity in the brain by a sort of evolutionary principle of the survival of the fittest connections. As with natural selection of gene pools, however, the real scientific problem is specifying the mechanisms by which 'fitness' affects survival. In other words, we are back with a functional explanation and need to study the particulars of the mental and physiological mechanisms of learning and memory in order to sort out how the brain really does it.

That is, the weakness of both functional and ontogenic accounts is that neither sort of explanation tells us how the system actually works. It is when we come to describing the mechanisms of the Müller-Lyer illusion that a distinction must be drawn between mind and brain, visual perception and visual neurones. Indeed, there are quite possibly one or more levels of mechanistic explanation between, variously called subpsychological, computational, integrative neurophysioligical, etc.

Considering neural mechanisms, i.e. the physical 'engineering' needed, there is, as far as I know, no direct evidence yet for a neurophysiology of size constancy. We are still having enough trouble getting the wiring diagram for shape recognition. (The theory of edge-detecting connections stated by the Nobel Prize-winning neurophysiologists Hubel and Weisel has not stood up to further investigation. Lines are as likely to be created by top - down interpretative strategies, like the late David Marr's "primal sketch"). In any case, a full description of a piece of engineering includes the jobs that the machinery manages to do; it doesn't just describe the overall functions achieved; it specifies how different subfunctions emerge from the physical machinery. This would be a cognitive but sub - psychological explanation, not the photic stimulation of the retina and the firing of neurones. This is a distinction between mental processes and physiological processes.

Many mental processes are not conscious. There is an ambiguity in the word "mind" in common usage and indeed within psychology too. Having something in mind is usually a claim to awareness of it, at least at some level some of the time. Nevertheless a great deal of what we do in our mind, for example rather out loud or on paper, just pops results into consciousness. In the case of the Müller-Lyer illusion, the effects of the arrow lines on length judgement may well never be accessible to awareness, although one can fight the illusion when one is alerted to it. (In fact my Lab book shows that I trained myself out of the illusion in about 3 dozen trials with feedback of errors. Coming to it 30 years later, I'm as susceptible as I ever was. Nevertheless, I'd probably learn to overcome it again more quickly, because memories stay stored away somewhere in our neuronal connections).

This brings us to one of the most important points about the science of the mind. It may not matter at all whether or not the mental processing is conscious for the psychologist's ability to work out how a performance of a task is achieved. We can diagnose what visual information is used and even how it is used, by varying different aspects of the diagram and recording what happens to judgements of line length that show the illusion. For example, if the strength of the illusion depended on the angle of the the arrowheads outside the range of angles involved in room perspective, that would cast doubt on the functional story and point to some dependence on orientation acuity perhaps.

Serial Learning

The second example comes from a very old, little Introduction to Experimental Psychology by the Birmingham educational psychologist C. W. Valentine, which had reached its fifth edition when I ran my first psychological experiments on myself when I was holed up in my rooms with a broken leg during my second term in Oxford as a chemistry undergraduate.

This procedure is still being used to investigate cognitive mechanisms of money. It involves going through a series of items trying to remember them and so is called "serial learning" (nothing to do with raising your IQ with vitamin-fortified cornflakes!) We ran through the procedure once during the meeting and saw the classic effects, before thinking about some testable explanations in terms of conscious or subconscious mental processing.

At this stage of my talk, I told the Conference that I would recite a dozen or so letters in turn and they should try to remember them all as best they could. I then read out a list of 17 different letters of the alphabet in a jumbled order, at a rate of about one per second. I used a monotone at the same loudness throughout, except for the tenth letter which I whispered.

Immediately I had finished, they started jotting down as many letters as they could remember, writing them in any order but without risking putting down letters I had not said. I gave 30 seconds and then went through the list writing down an estimate of the proportion of people who put up their hands to indicate that they had written down that letter. Nearly everybody got the first letter and almost as many the second, but fewer had recalled the third letter and little more than half got the 4th to 7th letters. Fewer than half had remembered the 8th, 9th, 11th and 12th letters, but three-quarters had written down the whispered 10th letter. The 13th letter was recalled by only a third, but more and more people had written down the remaining letters the nearer they were to the end, with about three-quarters remembering the last letter I had recited.

This is the classic finding of a bow-shaped curve of correct recall frequency. The good memory for the first items on the list is called the *primacy effect*. The good memory for the last items is called the *recency effect*.

The evidence from more detailed experiments on the conditions for good performance in this task is that a key mechanism involved is one or more forms of 'mental rehearsal'. Many participants in such an experiment can probably guess that from what they were deliberately trying to do as the list is recited. In modern jargon, we have a working memory of limited capacity. We can attend to only about 7 items, give or take a couple. If we wish, we can recycle a series of at most around 5 to 9 items, such as a telephone number.

Recent work from the MRC Applied Psychology Unit in the Other Place indicated that we rehearse by seeing them in the mind's eye or ear. The psychologists call these cognitive mechanisms articulatory, visual and auditory "codes". Objective evidence as to which mental process you were using, consciously or not, can be obtained from the reduction in your success when you get to rehearsing. (Note that these are experiments with the meaning of what is going in and out, not with mere physical interventions. Cutting off the fuel to an aero-engine or firing a lucky gunshot into it will not tell you whether it operates a propeller or a ram-jet: the evidence can only come from alterations of the specific conditions of propulsion, such as reducing the pressure of the air through which the plane is flying).

The '*primacy*' effect occurs because you can rehearse the first few items more often than items that come after your working memory has been filled. Maybe you put the letters into several different codes or onto duplicate lists in one code: again, we can design experiments which help to find out which. This will give more information to draw on after you can no longer rehearse those letters. You might feel more confident about the two or three letters that were first on the list.

The '*recency*' effect arises because the last letters were still in working memory when recall starts. Therefore they may well be the first letters recalled. They might seem clearer in the mind than other letters that had to be dragged from nonconscious memory. Indeed, writing the last few letters down would be just re-rehearsing them on paper instead of in the head. It might have been easier if the latter had been rehearsed in a handwriting code instead of an articulatory code, or if you were asked to remember the items by articulating them out loud instead of writing them down!

We can speculate about that "magic number" 7 (+/-2) as the capacity of short-term memory. Is that how the brain is in nature or in society? Is it the number of words in a spoken sentence? I suspect that it's all and none of these. They all may have something to do with it but the reason is deeper than any of those levels of analysis. Perhaps they are all requirements on the working memory of a highly versatile social animal who had to survive the challenges of hunting on the savannah. Between 5 and 9 chunks of usable information in attention might well emerge as appropriate for any finite intelligent system that uses focal processing, and such attentional or conscious work may be crucial to management of any complex intelligence.

The earliest work on artificial intelligence did not limit the size of the working memory used in the computer programs and in fact the programs were in list-processing languages. However, the programs were often very inefficient unless some control structure was added that reduced the number of items that were actively being processed at one stage in carrying out the task.

Now the rage in AI, and in theoretical psychology too, is for so-called neural networks. These are in fact nonlinear multivariate statistical packages. They are as different in principle as you could get from lists, with lots of parallel processing and not much serial processing (although simulations of both sorts of processing can in fact be programmed in each other's languages, which shows up again the issue of levels of explanation). The problem with these networks is that they have no initial structure. Worse, the structure of connections that they build to deal with a very particular problem cannot be used for other purposes or even accessed without adding other sorts of structure.

Real - life psychological investigation

Those two experiments should have begun to give a feel for how a carefully planned and interpreted investigation can read the human mind to some extent, even when the person is not aware of all the processes being used to achieve something.

For convenience, I have used very simple, dry and 'physical' tasks. Study of the workings of emotional moods, relationships between people or creative tasks, of course, has greater technical and even ethical difficulties. Yet the same basic paradigm can be used in attempts to diagnose how someone's mind is working in what they are doing and how they are reacting.

Indeed, we read each others' minds all the time. However, we may not be able to see far or very reliably into someone else's thoughts and feelings, let alone their subconscious, unless we know that person well and also know a bit about how people's minds work generally, and how people differ too.

Furthermore, we read our own minds by much the same publicly checkable techniques. Contrary to foundationalist philosophies, I have no certain knowledge of myself through private access to an inner world of consciousness. This introspectionalist fallacy still permeates our culture and infects even some psychologists today. Yet results from experimental psychology at the turn of the century cast serious doubt on introspection and it was finally debunked as a concept half a century ago by philosophers such as Popper, Wittgenstein and Ryle.

Nonetheless, how things seem to people and the way they state their views are invaluable evidence as to how they are thinking and feeling and indeed how they might behave in the situation of the discussion or being discussed. A major theme in my own research over the last decade has been an elaboration of the person - by - person approach that I mentioned starting with when I first got into psychology. I've always been keen on on studying the individual's performance, although I also group data from experiments and surveys as has become the norm in psychology since the rise of statistics to test agricultural trials. My research group has now developed ways of structuring open - ended conversation between an investigator and a respondent, with or without control of the physical context under discussion, so that we can measure a few of the particular mental processes that the individual is using in their statements. The same technique can be used on repeated behavioural observations without words, including on infants and members of other species.

Psychology is about how the mind works and that means it is about ordinary life. Laboratory studies are only psychological insofar as they tell us something about how our research participants go about their daily lives. The same is true of course about genetics, biochemistry and neuroscience.

Biochemistry of schizophrenia

So now let's turn from little experiments to two big human problems to which psychology is central. The first is a universal form of serious mental disorder.

It so happens that the first possible connection between chemistry and the mind that I came across was in the Bodley's Radcliffe Science Library. It was in several papers in what was then called the Journal of Mental Science and is now the British Journal of Psychiatry. This was an early speculation about the biochemical basis of the hallucinations and delusions that are common in the psychotic disorders that are called 'schizophrenia'. [The hallucinogenic drugs LSD and mescaline had some similarities in structure to breakdown products from some of the chemical transmitters across synapses between nerve cells that had recently been discovered in the brain.] As things turned out, I have so far done very little research directly on schizophrenia but I have kept in close touch with the literature and some of my teaching has been about mental disorder and its neuroscience.

It is widely agreed that one of the mechanisms contributing to schizophreniform psychoses involves the effects of over-activity of the neurotransmitter dopamine. Medications that block some of the actions of dopamine in the brain have at least a calming effect on agitated patients and so they are called major tranquillisers or neuroleptics. Some think that they work directly against the psychosis.

One can formulate a crude but not unrealistic neurophysiological theory of the role of dopamine in the auditory hallucinations, obtrusive thoughts and emotional pressure that are key schizophrenic symptoms. This neurotransmitter sets the tone of networks under the cortex in the forebrain that are basic to deciding what to do next, in action and in thought. That is, in cooperation with other transmitters such as GABA and acetylcholine, dopamine adjusts the background level of excitation of these decision networks.

If there is not enough excitation from dopamine, no decision comes out of the network. If this is in the movement network, that means we can't get started. This is a major symptom of Parkinson's Disease in which dopamine neurones die off.

If, on the other hand, there is too much excitation from dopamine, then too many options can get through the network. As a result, wrong as well as right decisions come out. If this is in the more cognitive part of the network (in the mesolimbic system under the temporal lobes), what is being heard or what should be believed or what really matters is misidentified. The sufferer becomes detached from reality. In some senses, emotion splits from reason, which is what the 'split mind' of 'schizo-phrenia' is (not multiple personality disorder).

There is no dispute that high tone and low tone would have these sorts of effects on the functioning of a laterally inhibited decision network in the nervous system. What is more controversial is that this is an important part of what has gone wrong underneath one or both of the temporal lobes in schizophrenia. Yet, even if this idea is along the right lines, does it simply that the right kind of anti-dopamine drug could cure schizophrenia?

I think not. By itself, the action of a drug cannot deconstruct a delusional system that has been built up or destroy specifically the memory of the voice that one heard giving an important message. This requires mental work and indeed social work, i.e. the reconstruction and maintenance of realistic relationships with other people and to the physical world as well perhaps.

On the other hand, though, society alone cannot 'unscrew' a 'screw-up' in the brain networks either. No amount of sympathetic family support can stop a bad psychotic break from crippling the sufferer while the symptoms are rampant.

Furthermore, this anguish of the soul has spiritual aspects. Indeed, schizophrenic delusions often are religious in content -not that the BBC is broadcasting messages into my head, but that the voice of God is speaking to me. This cuts both ways. British psychiatrists initially had problems with extrovert AfroCaribbeans who got into hospital and poured out their version of Rastafarian theology.

The *shaman* speaking with the voice of the spirits is highly regarded in some societies. The Jewish prophets, including Jesus himself, were sometimes regarded as mad even by their compatriots. All the same, most psychotic delusions are so wildly unrealistic and incoherent that no sane person could consider them to be a divine revelation. Yet a psychiatric diagnosis may not disqualify a religious authority. We are exhorted to try the spirits. We shall know them by their works.

Perhaps even nearer to home, it has been speculated that the human race has to carry genes for vulnerability to schizophrenia because they are the genes necessary for creativity and divergent intelligence. We've all heard of the idea that genius and madness are linked. However, I'm not aware of support for such ideas from family pedigrees or from the relevant psychology.

A more definite possibility (mentioned by Dr. Sloper) is that dopamine synaptic transmission is a part of normal pleasures and emotionality. The network theory above could implicate dopamine in psychological "energy" and also the intensity or meaningfulness with which some experiences or decisions can be permeated. If true, this could be part of how strongly one is moved by a Christian message or how clear a call to Christian service seems.

Indeed, some recent research into the context of schizophrenia has reported a 35% prevalence of experiences of unusually high sensory intensity. This is remarkably similar to the 35 - 50% who reported occasions giving them a sense of a presence or a power, such as when gazing at a sunset, in surveys of religious experience reviewed in the book by Dr. David Hay, former Director of the Alister Hardy Research Centre which is now here at Westminster College. Maybe the perception of God in the things he has made that the Creator has implanted in us all (Romans 1:20) depends on a high normal level of dopamine activity in the mesolimbic system...

A psychobiosocial approach to the pleasures of eating

The second illustrative issue comes from my main area of research, in which I've ended up working on biological, perceptual, motivational and social aspects since I switched to psychology departments in the mid-1960s. This is the most common cognitively complex behaviour we have, much neglected by psychologists though it be. I refer to eating, the purchase, preparation and consumption of food, what in our bodies and our culture influences our food choices, what impact food has on our health and our enjoyment of life and what foods and drinks mean to us as individuals and as communities.

That already says enough to signal my psychobiosocial unity-arianism! To be brief, I'll focus on an aspect where some fundamental discoveries have great practical importance. This is the role of eating habits in weight control and the prevention of life-threatening obesity.

As physical bodies, we are bound by thermodynamics, just like all the rest of the cosmos. The basic science of weight and shape is the law of conservation of energy. It does no good when members of the public and of healing professions get so mystical or carried away by hopes of the latest pill or potion that they ignore the fact that obesity is caused and cured only by the balance of energy taken in by eating and the energy spent normally as heat from metabolism and by physical activity. Weight gain can only come from eating more than needed, even very little on average over the years. Weight loss can be achieved only by eating less energy than is being used, although it does not have to be much less. The lost weight is kept off only by an energy intake not exceeding energy expenditure.

Unfortunately, however, some workers on 'fat physics' and the physiology of obesity regard energy balance as the only science and the rest as stamp-collecting. Fat people in rich countries are often presumed to be greedy, lazy and ill-disciplined. Some clinicians and indeed friends and relatives blame someone who does not get weight off for simply not trying hard enough. Even the person blames herself -and it is usually a woman who suffers this way, or even nowadays an 8- or 10-year-old girl, because the natural rounded and pear-shaped female figure is unfashionable in a youth-orientated and egalitarian culture. Going on a diet is a ritual self-immolation on the altar whose high-priestesses are the mannequins of *haute couture*. Dieting is usually an empty ritual because weight seldom stays off and the desired shape cannot be reached by those blessed with normal bones and hormones. So, as a result, we have the disorders of dieting, namely 'comfort eating' and other emotional misuse of food, bingeing and purging, and a loathing for normal fleshiness leading 15 or so of young women a year to self-starvation, ending fatally for a substantial minority.

Thus obesity is not just a physical phenomenon of energy imbalance. It is also a communal phenomenon of "shape chauvinism" and a psychological phenomenon of problems with self-image, emotional self-management and finding and keeping to the personally appropriate habits of eating, drinking and physical activity. The root of this problem in our society is that we move about less when we get into our 20s with a desk job, a car and no prolonged or vigorous exercise and yet we keep the sizes of meals and frequency of drinks and snacks that we needed when more active and perhaps growing still too.

Our research has pointed to some particularly fattening habits. These include some great British institutions such as: drinks and nibbles after supper; tea and biscuits (or a Coke and a Mars Bar) mid-morning and mid-afternoon; too much fat hidden in everything; and having calories in our puddings, instead of packing them into our first course, especially the starches and sugars.

This last trick (e.g. loading up with pasta or boiled potato) I've shown experimentally can help us learn to resist the temptation to take a lot of dessert that goes with that entree. Oddly enough, the first bit of brain research I did may well show a pathway by which emotions can disrupt this learned lack of interest in a dessert. So we come a full circle round from the sociology through the psychology to the neurobiology.

What psychology is not

I hope now that it is clearer how it is possible to be scientific about the mind of a human person. Psychology truly is the science (logos) of the soul (psuche) in the biblical Hebrew sense (and as Professor Young has assured us, the classical Greek sense too). This is the soul in the sense shared by all live animals, not an uniquely human faculty. Over a thousand souls perished as the Titanic went down. The soul is the dynamic within our intentional and involuntary behaviour, not the immortal self, the seat of consciousness or the 'ghost in the machine' variously understood by the Medieval Church, the Renaissance foundationalists and their followers to this day.

It should be clearer what the mind is not. Perhaps we can recognise psychology with Es now (sorry about the pun).

The mind is not the faculty of knowing

Psychology is *not* epistemology. The way we know things is not to exercise our minds in the correct way. No amount of confidence will make the colour - blind person right who believes that a green -painted letterbox is red. No amount of Christian assurance can establish that Christ was raised from the dead.

Knowing something is (roughly speaking) having a belief that it is true and having good reasons for that belief. Neither of these criteria involves the nature of our mental processes.

The mind is not the self

Psychology is not empathy with others or self-knowledge either. A counsellor's sensitivity to a client's needs and a person's search for insight are moral exercises, however much they may depend on empirical particulars or principles.

The mind is not consciousness

Psychology is not existential, nor does it deal with subjective data. This is the most pervasive misunderstanding of psychology among other scientists, and in medical and other professions, philosophy, theology, literature and thinking people generally, because it is deeply embedded in our high culture since at least the Renaissance. Cartesian body-mind dualism and the fallacy of introspection dominated the early decades of psychological science too. It was not at all exorcised by the behaviourists' move of denying the existence of mind. It still haunts some unreconstructed parts of experimental psychology such as psychophysics.

It's the approach of these people that is subjectivist, not the verbal data that they call subjective. In medical research, for instance, psychological matters are regarded to do with what is in the consciousness of the patient. Ratings of sensations, moods, attitudes or beliefs are treated subjectively, by taking the numbers as meaning just what the investigator means by the words attached to the numbers for the rater to use. No scientist takes the reading on a meter to be inherently meaningful in this way: what the meter-reading measures depends entirely on the objective performance of the instrument in producing the reading from the input as prepared by the user. So, similarly, a rating score and even the qualitative content of what people say is entirely objective evidence insofar as it can be shown to be the effect of some systematic influence on such output, either within a pattern of output or resulting from a known pattern of input.

Thus, for example, a sweetness rating can be used very simply and accurately to measure sugar concentration. We are even shown that a savoury taste can be recognised and indeed mimicked by a mixture of compounds tasting salty, sweet, sour and bitter. However, it is a much more complicated business (involving other chemical compounds and other ratings that all vary independently of sugar and sweetness levels) to measure the strength of a private sensation of sourness (or any other expressible content of consciousness), as distinct from being unaware of the taste of the acids in an apple as one enjoys eating.

The mind is not all obvious

Psychology is not dead easy -it's not all just common sense. Clearly we do know a lot about ourselves and other people, both from our own actions and observations and also from the conventional assumptions about people that the philosophers now call 'folk psychology'. However, the empirical theories that anybody may have about people in general or about a particular person, even her- or himself, are open to controlled testing, which is what psychology takes to be its task. (Our factual beliefs are also open to critical examination for conceptual coherence, which is what philosophers try to be good at, although it may also need scientific or historical expertise).

The mind is not the spirit

Psychology is not exegesis. Biblical anthropology and the Christian doctrine of human nature provide deep insights into the human condition, but they do not begin to answer the questions of modern science about what precisely influences what, in our thoughts and feelings. In O.T. Hebrew *nephesh*, the soul, is the life or behaviour of a communicative earthly being, and the N.T. Greek use of *psuche* is consistent with that. Spirit is a concept that may overlap but it has other uses, including for God's activity in the world and in human life. The empirical psychology of religion deals with the natural processes involved, even in a believer's devotional relations to the Lord, but biblical theology deals with the spiritual aspects of those relations.

What 'psychology' is the name of

By analogy with the science of physics or with physic, the old name for medicine, psychology could have been called physics or physic, but those terms were names for mediums and mesmerist entertainers when scientific study of the mind began in Germany 150 years ago. Physic became physiology and mental science became psychology, as also for example cosmology, geology, ecology, biology, zoology, anthropology and sociology. This however is a hijack of the '-ologies', because logos, or reason, is not confined to the search for empirical bases for generalised casual explanations but is a key part of any discipline. This includes theology, but mention of the 'queen of sciences' reminds us that *scientia* also means simply knowledge.

Some of the more laboratory-based psychologists have been unhappy with 'softer' meanings given to the word. So some experimental psychologists on the Continent and in the U.S.A. have taken on the name Psychonomics (Gk. *nomos*, law). This path was taken long ago by scientific observers of the stars, distinguishing astronomy from astrology.

Scientists of the mind have not established exclusive rights over the title 'psychologist' -yet, anyway. (The British Psychological Society now has a Register under its Royal Charter, so that only a scientifically-trained and specifically-qualified practitioner may legally use the title Chartered Psychologist). I don't think we can proscribe everyday uses of the word 'Psychology' that do not subject themselves to the disciplines of scientific method: I use the word myself in everyday talk when my expertise is not being invoked. I too talk with mystified horror about the mind of an IRA or UFF bomber and I am happy to chat about the psychology of the humour in a particular TV commercial.

Do please feel free to talk about 'biblical psychology', although I shall use the more common term 'biblical anthropology' for the scriptural doctrine of (hu)Man(ity). Nevertheless, there is a real and important distinction between psychology as a science and, for example, generalising literary accounts of the mind, philosophies of personality, or therapies for the human condition that do not open themselves fully to scientific investigation. That includes psychoanalysis and most of the writings of Freud and Jung, for example. I have to say that the criterion of research validation puts in question the motivational hierarchy of Abraham Maslow and a number of other systems that are popular in business circles.

This distinction might be sharpened if we called nonscientific approaches to the human mind 'Psychosophy' rather than psychology.

Applications of psychology

All sciences are fundamental disciplines, worthy of purely intellectual interest or, as Newton put it, thinking the Creator's thoughts after Him. Yet they all deal with some aspect of 'real life' and have practical applications. Indeed, too, each science raises value questions that they cannot answer from their own intellectual resources alone. At the very least, there are questions about allocation of economic resources for research in the field and for educating newcomers to it.

The science of the person, though, is about parts of real life that can be problematic to live through for large numbers of people. Relevant psychological understanding and practical experience, even though limited, may be able to help solve some problems or at least reduce or manage them. This might broadly be termed 'psychotherapy', although many psychotherapists are not trained in scientific psychology. Medically qualified practitioners who specialise in offering medication (chemotherapy) or expert advice (psychotherapy) to treat certain psychological problems (mental disorder) are called 'psychiatrists' (very few of whom are psychologists). However, both these titles have Greek roots that mean the 'cure of souls', which used to be the name for an exclusively religious ministry. Nevertheless, the Christian pastor and the family doctor have worked together for centuries. Furthermore, counsel and support to the psychologically troubled has been provided since time immemorial by experienced but unordained believers and by practitioners who are not medically qualified, let alone by family and friends (when they are not part of the problem). So psychotherapy shades into various forms of counselling and counselling shades into friendship.

Where does psychology as a science fit into the caring professions? An answer would go beyond my brief and take me much further overlength. Fortunately the 1995 conference of Christ and the Cosmos is planned to be on the Behavioural Sciences. I expect that some of the practical implications of psychology will be explored in depth then. Let me just conclude with an oversimplified tabulation of some of the areas of personal help and the therapies used by them. Perhaps that will serve as another sort of "taster" for 1995.

Personal work (human service) professions			**Personal therapies**
		P	
Social caseworkers		S	
Nurses		Y	
GPs	EXERCISE	C	Surgery / ECT
Consultants	HEALTH	H	Medication
Mental Health	CLINICAL	O	Stress / biofeedback
Mental handicap	EDUCATIONAL	L	Behavioural
Education	OCCUPATIONAL	O	Cognitive
Counselling	COUNSELING	G	
Ministers, friends, one's self		Y	Spiritual ministry

QUESTIONS following Professor Booth' Lecture

Q. **It would not be difficult to program a computer in such a way as to suggest that the computer had feelings and appeared to be making moral decisions. At what stage do you think that something like a computer could be said to have a soul or a mind or a spirit? Is the difference between a computer and an organic thing like a brain purely quantitative?**

A. The difference is not purely quantitative. If we are serious about the naturalness of the human mind, then we must allow the possibility that there are other forms of physical system that could be brought up and educated if they had the proper match between their physical organisation and the demands on them from their environment. This raises what I think is certainly not entirely a empirical question, but also a value question. For example, would a sufficiently efficient robot be a candidate for being seriously considered for legal status? If it ever happened, moral questions would arise of how we should treat this entity. Of course, there are big philosophical questions about what would count as having real feelings. John Searle is well known for putting up the Chinese Room example. He suggested that, even if a computer could use lists of Chinese words, an

English-Chinese dictionary and so on, so that it could communicate like a Chinaman without any Englishman being able to find it out, yet the computer would still not have a mind because it is not organic. That seems inconclusive to me. If we could build a computer that did behave exactly like a human being against all forms of test and analysis, then we should have to face the moral question of whether or not it did have some form of personality, whatever it was like under its silvery skin.

Q. **Could you explain in physiological terms what happens when you select a pattern of movement, and in what circumstances you should be regarded as responsible for having selected the pattern that you do select?**

A. A neurophysiologist or an exercise scientist could answer the first part of that question better than a psychologist. All I want to say is that there is a neurophysiology of motor control, explaining the movements of the muscles, limbs, and the rest of the body, including the larynx which produces the sounds of speech. You ask where responsibility lies in a system with this physical basis. The decision is made according to criteria which this individual system is using. A mechanistic system makes the input/output transformations itself. Obviously, in the human case where there are complicated representations, thoughts, interpretations and intentions which are reflected on by the system itself as well as being accessible from the outside. Other systems -I'm deliberately using nonpersonal language -are able to comment on the criteria which the deciding system is using. Thus there can be criticism, blame and praise. We have relevant ethical discussion between systems which are entirely mechanistic in themselves. The language of responsibility can at least have a coherent and effective role.

Q. **Is it possible to say whether my decision to tell you a lie can be explained entirely in terms of the neurones within my brain, or is some other factor involved?**

A. There is no way we can show how it is done at the present time.

Nevertheless I see no reason to suppose that we need to invoke extra things going on in the mind that are not dependent on the physical processes in the brain that have been informed and educated according to the criteria of our cultural tradition. The right or wrong a person does is as dependent on his upbringing and culture as on his brain and body, a psychologist would assume. Yet how the programming of rational, emotional and moral systems in the brain is done by our involvement with others in society is way beyond even the theorising of both neuroscience and cognitive psychology at the moment. Beyond such a scientific account of a person is of course the spiritual issue of what your intention to lie would do to your relationship to God.

Q. **Is it necessary for people to be somewhat abnormal in their behaviour in order to be geniuses?**

A. I suspect this is at least as much an historical question as a scientific one. It is very difficult to make a scientific study of creative genius, or for that matter the sort of madness that is not destructive, because they are relatively rare people and seldom recognised before fully formed. Genius is highly individualistic, too, and dependent on time and locality. So the answer to the question, if there is one, is likely to depend on the sort of genius and the conditions of the time.

A very simple model of creativity is the digging up of new things from the subconscious, or indeed from external sources, and having some criteria for recognising ones that might be more productive to pursue. The conscious critical part of intelligence, creativity and moral argument is having a modest enough number of principles that you can actually apply to whatever sort of new possibilities arise from the situation or the subconscious, to enable you to select what is nearer to right, or what is further from right. This model can be applied to the arts, to scientific discovery, and to moral development of societies and individuals. That is only a simple first attempt to structure a very complicated issue. As far as it goes, though, this model does not suggest a necessity for anything more abnormal for genius than a rich imagination and strong self-discipline.

Maybe anything more is at risk of being regarded as abnormal, though.

Q. **There are several things I want to put alongside one another, if I may.**

The first is that, when I taught mathematics, I used to be frustrated by how people tried to remember 'how to do' things. It would have been much better if they had learned how to feel free with the techniques, in order to be able to play with the problems they had been given, thus putting them into a form which they then recognised. Really worthwhile enterprise in this context is dealing with things in a form that you have never seen before, and actually producing results. How do you recognise that your results are right?

There is a second thought in my mind. I happened last year to go to a concert where the audience was lectured to by a Colonel of the Croatian army in battle dress, who also happened to be a moral philosopher. He was very keen to explain to us that ethnic cleansing was a natural, normal, sensible, creative way of behaving. In view of what you have said, that nurture and the scientific basis of perception in the brain provide the context for making judgements, are we obliged to recognise that there is no such thing as human moral judgement, but there is simply social and antisocial behaviour which is defined as good or bad according to the structure of society, the organisation of the brain in response to that, as well as the actual structure of the brain in physiological terms? On the basis of that, why should I bother to teach anybody mathematics?

A. As your last remarks indicated, I think that one way of addressing the problems you raise actually connects the two parts of what you say. We are in a real moral argument as well as a power struggle with the Serbs and Croats, and Bosnian Muslims too perhaps. By that I mean that the human race has to go through real historical and political processes, just as we as individuals undergo psychological development. Together, at our best attempt to reach an exchange of meaningful words and critical arguments that apply criteria of evaluation which a person may recognise even in a context other than the one which is natural to their own tradition of thought. This is also the politico-historical nature of science, and even, if I may say, in of mathematics! That doesn't mean that there are no objective elements in human argument. On the contrary, we have to go through the biological, psychological and social processes of opening ourselves to these sources of moral and empirical knowledge, and indeed personal empathy and physical power. I suppose a good teacher uses persuasion and personal influence to get people to acquire skills and use them both to generate and to criticise new possibilities. A statesman-like politician or other public servant presumably plays a similar role for his or her own people and their relations to outsiders.

The Beauty of The Cosmos and the Beauty of God

The Rt. Rev. Richard Harries

At one time the poet Wilfred Owen thought of being ordained. He even worked for a period as lay assistant in the Parish of Dunsden. It was not a happy time. When he left he intended to write to the Vicar giving reasons for his dissatisfaction. We do not know whether or not Wilfred Owen wrote that letter, but the draft, on the back of an envelope, was found among his papers after his death in France in 1918. It reads:

> "To Vicar ....., the Christian life affords no imagination, physical sensation, aesthetic philosophy."

The experience of Wilfred Owen can be paralleled many times over from both Protestant and Catholic sources. People have found the Christian faith too narrow in its sympathies, inimical to the feelings and stifling to the imagination. In short, it has seemed to afford them "no aesthetic philosophy". By this Owen meant no place for beauty, whether in the arts or nature. This is a disaster. For without an affirmation of beauty there can in the end be no faith and no God worth our love.

Beauty is one of those big words that modern philosophy tiptoes around. It is also a word that in ordinary conversation is liable to bring up so much gush, what T.S. Eliot termed "undisciplined squads of emotion", that most people are understandably reticent about its use. Moreover, because of our being, our understanding of life and who we are, people are extremely reluctant to placard their feelings in public.

The Importance of Beauty

The vast majority of us, however, are touched and moved by what strikes us as beautiful, especially in nature. Indeed, for many, it is the experience of the natural world which keeps them sane; which sustains and soothes them in a jarring world. Fishing is the most popular sport in the country, with over 4 million adherents. When I pass a fisherman (it seems to be mostly men) sitting for hour after hour on the river bank catching nothing,

I cannot believe that they are there just for the fishing. The water, the grass, the calm, the sky: all help bring peace of heart and mind. In recent years garden centres have been the growth areas and gardening is a major national pastime. Whether it is an allotment, a patio, a window-box or a flowerbed, millions of people find this direct contact with nature therapeutic. Millions more search for beautiful scenes; on car journeys they stop for views, they climb mountains, and go for walks. When Alyosha in Dostoevsky's novel 'The Brothers Karamazov' saw "the vault of heaven, full of soft shining stars, stretched vast and fathomless above him" he,

> "stood, gazed, and suddenly threw himself down on the earth. He did not know why he embraced it. He could not have told why he longed so irresistibly to kiss it, to kiss it all. But he kissed it weeping, sobbing and watering it with his tears, and vowed passionately to love it, to love it, and love it for ever and ever. 'Water the earth with the tears of your joy and love those tears' echoed in his soul."

Russians, some think, are given to this kind of emotional rapture, to extremes of feeling. Others of us are more restrained. But because people are private about what effects them most deeply, it should not be assumed that they do not, on occasion, share something of Alyosha's feelings about the beauty of the world.

C.S. Lewis, like Plato and innumerable philosophers influenced by him down the ages, believed that the longing aroused by beauty is a desire for what he called "our own far-off country", and said in speaking of this desire even now

> "I feel a certain shyness. I am almost committing an indecency. I am trying to rip open the inconsolable secret in each one of you -the secret that hurts so much that you take your revenge on it by calling it names like Nostagia and Romanticism and Adolescence; the secret also which pierces

> with such sweetness that when in very intimate conversation the mention of it become imminent, we grow awkward and effect to laugh at ourselves; the secret which we cannot hide and cannot tell, though we desire to do both."

What C.S. Lewis describes is an intense feeling, of the utmost significance to those who have experienced it in even a tiny way. If the Christian faith has no understanding of this or place for it, if it does not have an account of and a value for this sense which is so central to the hidden life of many (perhaps all), it is difficult to see how it can win our allegiance. Like Wilfred Owen we will walk away disgruntled, to write poetry or play music or paint, or simply to enjoy nature, seeing no connection between these activities which sustain and give meaning to our life and what we think of as religion.

Unless the experience of beauty in nature and the arts in encompassed and affirmed, the Christian faith will seem to have nothing of interest or importance to say. This is not, however, just a tactic to win the allegiance of the lost. The fact is that God is beautiful and the church is hiding this. This brings out an even more crucial reason why the concept of beauty must once again play a a central role in our understanding of the Christian faith. For without a positive theological evaluation of beauty there is no motive to delight God and no compelling reason to love him.

Faced with the statement, "You shall love the Lord your God", we can always reply "Why?" Being told to "love your neighbour", you can always say, "I choose to do this anyway." Being told that "there is a God who made heaven and earth", we can always shrug our shoulders and say, "So what?" The reason why believers do not make these responses is because we discern in God, the God whose love has shone in the face of Jesus Christ, that which is supremely beautiful. We are drawn, taken out of ourselves, by the one to whom St Augustine addressed the words: "Late have I loved you, beauty so old and so new." St Augustine was talking about spiritual beauty, the beauty of sublime, self-giving love. But it is central to Christianity, properly understood, that there is a resemblance, a relationship, in the arts, in a genuinely good person and in God; and that which tantalises, beckons and calls us in beauty has its origin in God himself. So as Hans Urs Von Balthasar, the one great modern theologian who has placed beauty at the centre of his theology, puts it:

> "We can be sure that whoever sneers at her name as if she were the ornament of a bourgeoisie past -whether he admits it or not -can no longer pray and soon will be no longer able to love."

That sentence is no exaggeration. A sense of beauty and its value, which can of course be part of the experience of the most unlettered person, is an indispensable prerequisite of love and power.

What is beauty?

If we look at a great painting, say 'The Baptism of Christ' by Piero della Francesca in the National Gallery, it is possible to pick out certain characteristics that contribute to its beauty. It has, for example, a delectable harmony. Most obviously there are vertical and horizontal lines that intersect at right angles. The tree, Christ, his praying hands, the water flowing from the bowl, the beak of the dove, and John the Baptist's right leg carry the eye up and down the picture. The hands of the angels and John the Baptist, the wings of the dove and the clouds in the sky float the eyes sideways and intersect the vertical lines at a number of points. But a series of right angles would be of little visual interest, so there are also harmoniously balanced diagonals, formed by the left leg of John the Baptist, the back of the man undressing, the silhouette of the hills and so on. Again, if the picture was divided down the middle it would be dull, but the artist wished to have different sections. So the position of the tree makes the actual baptism the major focus, whilst the space in the sector is related in a proportionate way to that behind the tree where the angels stand. An analysis of the blends and contrasts of colours could also be carried out by showing how they fit together in an interesting and arresting whole. In short, in every aspect there is harmony, balance, proportion; what ancient writers called symmetry and measure.

At the same time, the painting as a whole adds up to a satisfying unity, but again in a way which is no stereotype. The curve at the top of the painting, the leaves of the tree, and the combination of trees and water, combine to make the details cohere. The parts balance one another and contribute to the whole.

There is another feature we can easily recognise -the use of light. The body of Christ and the flesh tones of the other people in the picture have an extraordinary translucence. Similarly, the bark of the tree, the water and the sky stand out in an almost unearthly light. There is, we might say, a radiance about the scene.

Not every painting or work of art yields so easily to this analysis. Nevertheless, it is easy to understand why St. Thomas Aquinas (1225 - 74), selected wholeness, harmony and radiance as the three defining characteristics of what is beautiful. For these are the three most obvious characteristics that emerge whether we look at a classical work like Piero della Francesca's 'The Baptism of Christ' or a modern one like Bridget Riley's 'Daybreak'. They are characteristics that are applicable to sculpture and architecture as they are to painting. This understanding is one that draws on the long tradition of classical and Christian thinking on that subject. Richard Grosseteste, Bishop of Lincoln and scholar with a wide range of interests who, like Thomas Aquinas, lived in the 13th century, had this conception of beauty:

> "For beauty is a concordance and fittingness of a thing to itself and all of its individual parts to themselves and to each other and to the whole, and of that whole to all things."

The example of a painting has been given in order to show the strength of Aquinas' understanding of beauty as that which has wholeness, harmony and radiance. But every work of art has form of one kind or another.

Poetry makes use of metre, rhythm and rhyme; a novel has a beginning, a middle and an end, and a host of subtle interconnections, parallels, echoes and contrasts in the text. And so on. Forms can and do change, as when Wilfred Owen made more use of half-rhythms, assonance and internal rhyming, as when Hopkins developed his sprung rhythm, and Eliot reacted against Georgian poetry. But form there must be and without form there is no work of art. Forms vary enormously. But it is form which distinguishes a painting from a splurge of paint, music from cacophony of sound, a novel or a play from a rambling anecdote. In them all, the details relate to one another and the whole in a way which achieves a satisfying unity. There is a wholeness and harmony.

I recognise that for some the emphasis on wholeness, harmony and radiance will point to what is pretty rather than what is beautiful. For beautiful works of art often include that which is disturbing and ugly, dark and disruptive. They can express violence, evoke sorrow and depict the sordid. This is an important point which I fully accept. There is a world of difference between superficial prettifying and genuine beauty. But beauty must be beauty, must always be seen in integral relation to truth. It is this which allows it to express or include all that seems the opposite of what is whole, harmonious and radiant. But for the sake of clarity of terms I believe the word 'beauty' should be associated with the particular characteristics of form that I have outlined: wholeness and harmony.

Divine Glory

The poet W.B. Yeats wrote about a "Terrible Beauty". William Blake, in describing the awe - ful quality of a tiger's breath, wrote of a "fearful symmetry". These paradoxical phrases bring out the point that beauty is very different from mere prettiness. In some contexts the word 'beauty', by itself, seems to weak to convey the powerful impact a work of art or scene in nature has made on us. An accomplished performance of King Lear encompasses suffering and tragedy. So do many works of art, the paintings of Goya and the Passion music of Bach, to give just two

examples.
Constable wrote that there are two faults to be avoided in painting. One is "the absurdity of imitation" and the other is "bravura" -which he defined as "going beyond the truth". It is the truth of a landscape that the artist is trying to get at. This means avoiding all copying, either of works of art or of what is before the eyes, as though a photograph is being produced. It also means opening the eyes to try to see what is actually there, without imposing our own illusions and fantasies on it. Sometimes, in order to sell his pictures, Constable put in a little of what he called "eye-salve". But he was well aware of what he was doing and that this was a departure from the highest standards of artistic integrity which he set himself.

In 1826 he painted his famous landscape 'The Cornfield'. It shows a lane leading to a cornfield, the wind blowing in the sky, the trees and the corn. Also in the picture is a sheepdog, sheep and a boy picking a flower. "I do hope to sell this present picture -as it has certainly got a little more eye-salve than I usually condescend to give them."

All forms of art are in the business of truth; truth of eye and ear and mind. True beauty is inseparable from the quest for truth. When the attempt to produce something beautiful is separated from truth, the result is sentimentality.

It is well-known that Rembrandt went through a series of crises in his life, personal and financial, as a result of which his art radically changed its character. This is particularly noticeable in the way that he switched from grandiose descriptions of Biblical scenes to ones in which Jesus is depicted in a much more human, lowly manner:

> "Rembrandt finally turned his back on the glorification of man which had become a classical ideal, and which reached its zenith in Baroque art. Thus he shows us that he learned that it is a humble thing to be a man. From this time the beautiful ceased to be an end in itself for him. He realised that beauty must serve something higher, namely, truth, or

> else it is in danger of becoming an empty shell, falsifying the reality of life. If beauty accepts this part, it requires a new substance through which the eternal shines."

The attempt to get at the truth of things in this way is inseparable from certain moral qualities. Artistic integrity is the most obvious quality that is required. Here we come across the fact that sometimes an artist may be all over the place in their private lives whilst still producing works of great quality. This is because, whatever the mess in the rest of their life, they are still totally committed to their work, brooking no compromises. Patrick White describes such an artist in his novel 'The Vivisector'. The artist's moral life is totally at sea. But he is haunted by a vision that he strives and strives to produce on canvas. He is totally serious about this, utterly given over to the task.

Hopkins once wrote to Robert Bridges to say that "a kind of touchstone of the highest or most living art is seriousness; not a gravity, but the being in earnest with your subject -reality". He then went on to remark that some of the most famous works of art are not really in earnest and he instanced Roman literature. One of the reasons that the philosopher Ludwig Wittgenstein fell out with Bertrand Russell was that Wittgenstein felt Russell was not fundamentally serious, even about mathematical logic. Such fierce integrity is usually very difficult to live with.

The relationship between moral truth and beauty is a puzzling one. But they cannot in the end be separated. This comes out very clearly in the feelings of some war photographers to their work. In a television programme, 'Stains of War', a photographer, George Roger, spoke about his visit to Belsen after the war and his professional work, arranging beautiful compositions of the dead. Approached by a prisoner who tried to talk to him, but fell dead at his feet from weakness, Roger was positioning himself for a good angle on the corpse when he suddenly thought: "My God, what's happening to me?" He never undertook military assignments again.

All the photographers who took part in the programme felt that their work has coarsened their feelings. Larry Burrows, famous for his images from Vietnam, wondered "whether it was right to capitalise on the grief of others". Fouad Khoury, working in the Lebanon, found an editor's demand, "Don't you have any carbonised heads on the pavement?" too much, and gave it up.

The photographers felt there was an irreconcilable clash between aesthetic considerations and decent human feeling, between arousing interest in the readers of magazines and newspapers and proper feelings of shock and revulsion. Yet war photographers, like doctors, have a work to do. They need to keep the public informed of what is happening. Sometimes, as in the case of photographs from the Vietnam War, they play a vital role in arousing the revulsion and opposition of people at home to the war. Yet if the pictures are too shocking and revolting, readers will not be pleased and magazine editors will not in the end publish them. People like to feel a mild sense of outrage or pity. So pictures inevitably have a beautifying element to them, which makes them acceptable. They report the brutal truth but not in too brutal a way. There is a dilemma here which does not lend itself to simplistic solutions.

Eternal Wisdom

The concept of God as eternal wisdom is central to my theme for three reasons. First, wisdom is, according to the Scriptures, beautiful; secondly, because the marks of this beauty are proportion and measure, harmony and wholeness; and thirdly, because moral wisdom is integrally linked to those characteristics of beauty and order. In short, the characteristics of wisdom are akin to those of divine glory, considered as a sublime conjunction of beauty, truth and goodness. The difference is this: in divine glory it is the majestic splendour of God's love, truth and beauty that is set forth. With eternal wisdom it is the ordered beauty of the universe and the ordered beauty of our lives when they are lived at one with the divine purpose for them that is seen.

First, the beauty of wisdom. In the *Wisdom of Solomon* (7:25 - 82) in the Apocrypha, wisdom is described in these words:

For she is a breath of the power of God,
And a pure emanation of the glory of the Almighty;
Therefore nothing defiled gains entrance into her.
For she is a reflection of eternal light,
A spotless mirror of the working of God,
And an image of his goodness.
Though she is but one, she can do all things,
And while remaining in herself, she renews all things;
In every generation she passes into holy souls
And makes them friends of God, and prophets;
For God loves nothing so much as the man who lives with wisdom.
For she is more beautiful than the sun,
And excels every constellation of the stars.
Compared with the light she is found to be superior,
For it is succeeded by the night,
But against wisdom evil does not prevail.
She reaches mightily from one end of the earth to the other,
And she order all things well.
I loved her and sought her from my youth,
And I desire to take her for my bride,
And I become enamoured of her beauty.

This wonderful passage hardly needs comment. But we notice that the relationship between wisdom and God is akin to that between the word and God as described in the Prologue of John's Gospel; that the beauty of wisdom is such that we are "enamoured of her beauty", and that her work is that of "ordering" the universe and our lives.

This leads on to the second characteristic of wisdom. As that passage puts it, "She reaches mightily from one end of the earth to the other, and she orders all things well." Form is basic to all beauty; balance, proportion, pattern, all we mean by wholeness and harmony. In the beginning was chaos. "The earth was without form and void" (*Genesis 1:2*). But the Spirit of God breathed on this formlessness and gave the universe shape. Indeed, strictly speaking, creation and the structures of creation are inseparable. So it is that when we look at a crystal or a leaf we are captivated and awestruck by the patterns we discern. At every point in the universe such patterns can be seen, at the sub-atomic level, in atoms, molecules, cells and multi-cellular structures; in the microcosm and the macrocosm we see wonder and form. Indeed, we can only grasp intellectually what is there by depicting the unimaginable complexity of the world in forms, at the most basic level in mathematical forms. These structures and patterns of the universe reflect the work of eternal wisdom. Speaking to wisdom the writer of the Wisdom of Solomon continues in 11:20, "Thou hast arranged all my measure and number and weight". Mediaeval writers took this text and theme to be aesthetic as well as scientific and related both dimensions to the goodness of all that exists. The amazing variety and beauty of creation, held together beneath its multiple forms by an underlying unity, never ceased to make them marvel. As Umberto Eco puts it:

> "There was not a single mediaeval writer who did not turn this theme of the polyphony of the universe; and we find often enough that along with the calm and control of philosophical language there sounded a cry of ecstatic joy: "when you consider the order and magnificence of the universe... you will find it to be like a most beautiful canticle ... and the wondrous variety of its creatures to be a symphony of joy and harmony to very excess."
> (*William of Auvergne, De Anima V.18.*)

Quite a number of concepts were constructed in order to give philosophical expression to this aesthetic vision of the universe. But they all derived ultimately from the triad of terms given in the Book of Wisdom: number (*numerus*), weight (*pondus*), and measure (*mensura*).

Amongst modern writers it is Simone Weil who assumes the closest connection between order and beauty. Indeed, sometimes she seems almost to equate the two. When discussing beauty as a form of the implicit love of God, she heads the section: "Love of the Order of the World". Elsewhere she writes,

> "The subject of science is the beautiful (that is to say, order, proportion, harmony) in so far as it is suprasensible and necessary."

The third characteristic of eternal wisdom is the way our lives, when truly ordered, share in and reflect this wisdom. One of the unfortunate characteristics of the modern world is the way we have split asunder thinking, feeling and morality. Beauty is too often thought of simply in terms of emotional response. Conscience is usually understood to be a feeling of guilt, whilst pure hard thinking is reserved for science. In contrast to this rending apart of feeling, thinking and morality, our Christian forebears had a unified vision in which mental processes always had a role to play, and beauty was an aspect of objective reality. This is in no way meant to denigrate feeling. Mediaeval people felt just as strongly, if not more so, than we do. Nor is this to undervalue any light that psychology might throw on the judgements we make. But we have been created by God with minds. Conscience, for Thomas Aquinas, is not a matter of feeling, but of rational judgement: it is the mind making moral decisions. It is a matter of thinking hard about what in any circumstance is the right course of action in the light of fundamental Christian principles.

One of the characteristic features of all wisdom literature is the conviction that right action in the eyes of God is an essentially rational activity. It is sensible to act justly because that will lead to the well-being of oneself as well as of other people. At its worst this kind of moral teaching can seem simply prudential, doing good in order to prosper; or it can come across as banal or simply untrue. Good behaviour does not automatically lead to prosperity all round. But the vital element in this tradition is the conviction that God wants his world to flourish, and he has given us minds to enter into his divine purpose. We can use our minds to grasp his wisdom. In so ordering our lives aright, we will reflect the divine wisdom and in this we will also discern something of the divine beauty.

The unity of beauty, right ordering and moral wisdom is well seen in the work of the 6th century philosopher Boethius, who influenced many Christian writers in the Middle Ages, especially Dante. Boethius wrote:

In regular harmony
The world moves through its changes;
Seas in competition with each other
Are held in balance by eternal laws
Phoebus brings rosy dawns
In his golden chariot
That his sister Phoebe may rule the nights
That Hesperus brings;
The ways of the greedy sea
Are kept within fixed bounds,
Nor may the land move out
And extend its limits.
What binds all things to order,
Governing earth and sea and sky
Is love.
If love's reins slackened
All things held now by mutual love
At once would fall into warring with each other,
Striving to wreck that engine of the world
Which now they drive
In mutual trust with motion beautiful.
And love joins peoples too
By a sacred bond
And ties the knot of holy matrimony
That binds chaste lovers,
Joins too with its law
All faithful comrades.

O happy band of men,
If the love that rules the stars
May also rule your hearts!

In this vision of the order of the universe, the rhythm of the natural world is an expression of love. That love is also to be expressed in the ordered beauty of our lives.

With some trepidation I now say something about what science suggests about the physical universe we inhabit. My maths and physics did not go much beyond 'A' level, and that was so many years ago I can hardly add up. But there seems to me one basic point with which anyone can agree: the physical universe yields its secrets only to rational minds. Or, to put it the other way round, rational minds exploring the mystery of matter, space and time will grasp only what can be rationally structured.

When we explore the basic elements of which the universe is made up, we cannot see anything. There is nothing there that we can literally draw or picture. There are patterns of energy, relationships between the different elements involved, which we can symbolise and structure in terms of certain mathematical formulae. The same is true when we turn our gaze away from the microcosm to the macrocosm. We cannot see or literally describe what is happening at the outer edge of space. But we can give an account of what is happening with the use of certain mathematical equations.

These equations, these formulae in which the relationship between the elements involved are set out, all have form. They partake of "law", that is, they indicate certain patterns, observed regularities on the base of which predictions can be made. They are characterised by pattern, structure, symmetry; in short, they bear the marks of beauty as I have earlier outlined it.

This beauty is not just in the mind. It maps the universe as it is. Only rational minds can grasp what is there, but what they grasp really is there.

Perhaps beyond what the mind now grasps there is only total chaos. If so, the mind will never know, for such chaos cannot be rationally comprehended. The mind of its very nature structures experience. These structures, mathematical formulae that are at once endlessly complex and utterly simple not only account for a wide range of phenomena, they allow predictions to be made about how things are likely to behave. In short, they can be tested.

Professor Roger Penrose, Rouse Ball Professor of Mathematics here in Oxford, set out the aim of his first Gifford Lecture last year to give the picture that modern physics provides in describing the physical world at macroscopic level. He wrote of the "extraordinary accuracy of the appropriate theories - Newton's, Maxwell's, and Einstein's -as well as their mathematical elegance, will also be stressed." He makes two points. First the extraordinary accuracy of the appropriate theories. In short, their capacity actually to account for the way the world is and is likely to go. Secondly, their elegance.

Professor John Leslie has recently written; "Science once classified light, electricity and magnetism as separate factors. Then, seeking beauty in his equations, Maxwell unified all three." We note the reference to beauty. Leslie, in discussing a new book by Stephen Weinberg, dreams of a final theory, writes, summing up Weinberg's views:

> "What would be the signs of correctness in a speculative theory of everything? Beauty would be among them. Beauty is partly a matter of symmetries; roughly speaking, similarities between forces and particles of different types, and between ways in which the world looks to different observers .... Already 'there are symmetry principles that dictate the very existence of all the known forces of nature'."

We might note also, that the very quest for a totally unified set of principles, a theory of everything, is the quest for an ultimate unity and harmony, an

utterly complex simplicity, in which beauty may be said to reside.
Many scientists and philosophers have seen the order that lies at the heart of the universe as a kind of music. Kepler wrote:

> "Thus the heavenly motions are nothing but a kind of perennial concert, rational rather than audible or vocal.... Thus there is no marvel greater or more sublime than the rules of singing in harmony together in several parts, unknown to the ancients but at last discovered by man, the ape of his creator; so that, through the skillful symphony of many voices, he should actually conjure up in a short part of an hour the vision of the world's total perpetuity in time; and that, in the sweetest sense of bliss enjoyed through music, the echo of God, he should almost reach the contentment which God the maker has in his own works."

Karl Popper, from whom this quotation comes, himself remarks that

> "a great work of music (like a great scientific theory) is a cosmos imposed upon a chaos -in its tensions and harmonies, inexhaustible even for its creator".

Earlier I referred to the biblical theme of creation being the creation of form out of formlessness, pattern out of anarchy, creation out of chaos.

What the quotation by Kepler brings out so well is the way that different parts combine to bring about a pleasing whole. There is also another aspect of music which makes it a particularly apt analogy for understanding the work of God in creation, and that is the way the fixed elements and the innovative combine to bring about that which we respond to as something creative. As Arthur Peacocke has written:

> "In music new melodies and developments emerge intelligibly, yet inventively, out of earlier themes and fragments; and similarly in the processes of the world new

> forms develop, often surprisingly though post hoc intelligibly in the light of the sciences, from what precedes them."

In evolution it appears that it is the culmination of chance and necessity that makes possible the emergence of new higher forms of life. Chance, through random mutation, acting upon the given elements of the natural world allow for both continuity and change, the culmination of both bringing about the world we know. Music can be an analogy of this, because there also there is an elaboration of simpler units according according to often conventional rules intermingled with much spontaneity, surprise even. So, as Arthur Peacocke has written:

> "God as creator we might now see as composer who, beginning with an arrangement of notes in an apparently simple subject, elaborates it and expands it into a fugue by a variety of devices of fragmentation, augmentation and re-association .... Thus does a J.S. Bach create a complex and interlocking harmonious fusion of his seminal material, both through time and at any particular instant, which beautiful in its elaboration, only reaches its consummation when all the threads have been drawn into the return to the home key of the last few bars -the key to the initial melody whose potential elaboration was conceived in the moment it was first expounded .... Thus might the creator be imagined to enable to be unfolded the potentialities of the universe which he himself has given it, nurturing by his redemptive and providential actions those that are to come to fruition in community of free beings -an improviser of unsurpassed ingenuity."

The words from William of Auvergne, quoted above by Umberto Eco, show how easily people then thought of the order of the universe as a kind of music. This view does not only belong to the past. The mathematical models devised to map the foundation of the universe have a beauty about them which is akin to music. The young Ludwig Wittgenstein praised Bertrand Russell's work in such terms:

> "He spoke with great feeling about the beauty of *Principio*, and said -what was the highest praise he could give it - that it was like music."

And the relationship between music and spiritual reality has often been suggested.

Christ is the wisdom of God because his being is one with God and in the Incarnation he lived out his life in an unbroken union with his heavenly Father. The glory of God in Christ was for the most part hidden. The wisdom of God in Christ contradicted the standards of the world. Yet in him is eternal wisdom, the wisdom and love that made the stars. Christ takes our lives into God and orders them in a pattern of beauty. He is seeking to win over all people, to draw them to the beauteous fount of their being, the glorious goal of their longing. He is the crucified Lord of the Dance whose music can still be heard,

"They cut me down and I leapt up high,
I am the life that'll never, never die;
I'll live in you if you live in me;
I am the Lord of the Dance", said he.

The concept of wisdom needs to come more to the fore in Christian thought and practice today. It was of crucial importance for the early Church and its position needs to be recovered. For wisdom holds together what we are always in danger of splitting asunder -beauty, rational order and goodness. God is beautiful. "She is more beautiful than the sun." This beauty is expressed in the rhythms, patterns and structures of the universe. It is also to be reflected in the right ordering of our lives. When our lives are at one with the purpose of God for us, when we hear the divine music and join in the dance, we too have an ordered beauty. In and through wisdom God, the material world and the way we live are brought together. Aesthetics, rationality and morality are joined. Scientific exploration, artistic creation and behaviour exhibit the same characteristic of beauty, order and rationality. All can be referred to in terms of music and dancing.

QUESTIONS following Bishop Harries' Lecture

Q. **Beauty is very cultural. If the Church has had trouble in dealing with beauty, is that because it has had trouble coming to terms with culture?**

A. I quite agree that the church has had a great deal of trouble in coping with culture. But though, of course, you are right in saying that our understanding of what is beautiful is culturally shaped, I believe it is wrong to think that beauty is simply in the eye of the beholder, that is, all entirely relative. It is extraordinary how certain works of art and features of nature appeal to people of all cultures. Show me anyone in the world who does not appreciate the Taj Mahal. The Japanese understanding of nature does have a peculiar delicacy, but we can understand and enter into a Japanese appreciation of the beauty of nature. Although what is beautiful in other cultures can sometimes shock us so we do wonder whether it does radically differ from culture to culture, I do think that we can actually be educated into another culture's understanding of beauty in the same way that you can be educated into your own culture's understanding of beauty. For example, Japanese theatre strikes most people in the west as pretty strange, but it is actually possible to begin to appreciate it. In the same way that moral concepts are culturally shaped and therefore in certain respects seem to differ from culture to culture, the very fact that we have entered into dialogue with people from other cultures about both the nature of morality and the nature of beauty seems to suggest areas of common ground. The very possibility of discourse points to that which is in common.

Q. **The way we understand the universe at large is limited by the rational function of our brains. Is it not possible that our**

understanding of beauty is also a function of the way our brains are put together that beauty is merely an artefact of the way our brains work, and has no reality in its own right?

A. It is a function of the mind, and no doubt in part it is also a function of the brain, though I don't particularly want to discuss the relationship between the two at the present. I was stressing that beauty is a function of the mind. A scientific exploration of the universe actually maps out what is there. It is not simply an imposition by the mind or brain, but is actually a response to what is really there. We know that to be so because we can make predictions on the basis of those maps or formulae. I believe that the same is true also in our understanding of beauty. We are responding to what is there, though of course it can't be tested in the same kind of way.

Q. **Can one come to be persuaded that something which one thought to be beautiful isn't beautiful really? Is there a sense in which our generation has found that about God?**

A. It is certainly true that our understanding of what is beautiful can change. I happened to go round a tourist shop with my sister yesterday because she wanted to buy a present. Part of the shop was given over to paintings. She and I both reacted against paintings which were so obviously designed to meet the specifications of a particular kind of beauty -pastiche pictures of horses, rivers, mountains, sunlight -selling for about £500 too! They had clearly been designed for a very stereotyped understanding of beauty.

What is the case with most of us is that the kind of beauty we appreciate first of all is a beauty of a fairly obvious conventional kind. As we mature we move away from that in order to appreciate beauty of a rather more subtle and sophisticated, and in the end true, kind. I don't think, however, that people have turned away from God because they have changed their apprehension of what is beautiful. I think that one of the reasons they have turned away from God is that we have quite simply not put before people the beauty of God. I think it is is as simple as that. We have put before them often that which is morally revolting, rigid, moralistic, unattractive. This is in part because of the great neglect of the concept of the beauty of God. In Protestant theology the total neglect of it, but also in Catholic theology. It is interesting that von Balthasar in his great books very often focuses upon lay people, people like Gerard Manley Hopkins, Pascal, Peguy and so on. He doesn't go to Dante or many theologians, but rather to poets and other writers.

If we go to the Bible, all the way through the Hebrew scriptures there is central to it the concept of the glory of God. And the glory of God must include all that we mean by beauty. It is more than beauty. It is a sublime conjunction of beauty, truth and goodness. But it certainly includes all that we mean by beauty. The Christian scriptures say, "The God who said, 'Let there be light,' has shone in our hearts to give us the light of the glory of God in the face of Jesus Christ." Unless the church conveys something of that sense of the haunting beauty and glory of God, why on earth should people be attracted to believe and respond?

Q. **I visited St. Paul's cathedral and found it impossible to be reverent because of the noise and confusion. I went to the National Gallery and found people speaking in hushed tones before Francesca's painting of the Nativity. Art can sometimes succeed where religion fails.**

A. I entirely affirm what you have said.

Comment from the floor: I'm struck by the most incredible beauty I see sometimes in ugliness in some of the human beings I have to work with or look after. I'm thinking of people with severe autistic disorders, who behave in most ugly ways and may appear ugly, but may have the most extraordinary gift, like being able to play music by ear or to recite a piece of poetry having heard it only once, so-called ideo-savants, people who have the most exquisite beauty inside them. When I look at a grotesquely disfigured, mentally handicapped adult, dribbling and drooling, grunting and squeaking, which is an ugly and distasteful experience to behold, I see there in that person a tiny infant, as indeed Christ was a tiny infant. There I see the broken body of the Lord before me. Then when I see a speech therapist or a communication therapist using those pre-verbal grunts and gestures as a language and as music, there is seen an elegance which begins to develop. And we know that from that very primitive arrest in development new neural pathways can open up, and this severely-handicapped person can be brought on very slowly to achieve more and more, even to get up and walk, not by any flash miracle, but through human love. That is the crowning glory of God's beauty, the love between humans which was demonstrated by our Lord.

Q. **It is said that in about 150 years time a meteorite is expected to approach earth, possibly colliding with it and causing 100,000 deaths. The created universe is seen to be beautiful in its course, but the effects of such events are far from beautiful.**

A. It is of the very essence of creation that God lets things be, whether they are atoms, molecules, cells, multi-cellular structures, earthquakes, volcanoes, revolving planets or whatever. God cannot let things be on the one hand, which is what it is to create and give things a life of their own, and as it were hold them back. The problem you are raising is the same problem that runs through the whole of the created order. The fact of the matter is, as Austen Farrer once put it, God has chosen to weave the world from the bottom upwards, by a series of infinitely complex, interlocking forces. That is the way creation has come about.

The Temple of the Holy Spirit - on being embodied

Professor Frances Young

Anyone who had any lingering hopes that their real self might be a discrete immortal soul lodged somewhere in their body will probably have been disillusioned by this conference (though unfortunately I can't be sure since I've not been able to be present until now). My disillusionment with soul body dualism came a long time ago, and there were two sources. It's worth beginning by looking at these non-scientific challenges to the tradition in popular piety with which I had grown up.

The first arose from theological exploration. When I was a student, one of the unquestioned assumptions of New Testament and early Christian studies was that you could distinguish between Hellenic and Hebraic culture. The Hebraic ideas of the Bible were Hellenised by early Christianity, which expressed itself in Greek and took over the categories of Greek philosophy. To strip away these Greek accretions was to get back to Biblical truth. One classic example was the dichotomy between soul and body. This Platonic notion had nothing to do with Biblical ideas of the human person, it was said. The Hebrew Bible has no equivalent to the Greek psyche in the sense of an immortal soul. Rather God formed the human being from moistened dust, a story no doubt inspired by the myriads of clay figurines which we now know from every museum with an Ancient Near Eastern section, and then breathed life into the image thus created. At death, the divine spirit or breath returned to its divine source, and the dust reverted to the dust. A shade of the once living person might persist in Sheol, the grave or the underworld, but God's power did not reach down there (Ps.139:8 is the isolated exception that proves the rule!). When ideas of an afterlife began to emerge, and they hardly did before the Intertestamental period, it was a conception of resurrection that arose naturally from this understanding: God raised up the remains from the grave, re-created the clay figure, breathed new life into it. There was no doctrine of the immortality of the soul, and so, it was argued, a clear distinction should be made between the Hebraic notion of resurrection and the Hellenic concept of immortality.

The other consequence of this analysis was the convenient assertion that the Bible taught that a human person was a psychosomatic whole - convenient, since this 'whole person' idea of human being was thought to be more in accord with modern scientific understanding than the foreign Greek idea which had unfortunately got imported into Christianity. The long history of denigration of the body, the puritanical tradition, the idealisation of asceticism and celibacy - all this was not natural to the Judaeo-Christian tradition, but an unfortunate aberration. So this kind of thinking encouraged the 'this-worldly' revolution that has taken place in 20th Century Christianity. No longer did we have that "charge to keep", "a never-dying soul to save and fit it for the sky"; we were only "to serve the present age". The dichotomy between physical and spiritual, soul and body, could no longer be sustained on theological grounds. How convenient, given that science had turned the soul into an improbable "ghost in a machine", to plunder Koestler's clever phrase.

The second challenge was Arthur. As readers of **Face to Face** and the **Methodist Recorder** will be aware, Arthur is my adult son with severe mental disabilities. It doesn't take some elaborate scientific theory to prove to me that Arthur's personality is inseparable from his limited brain function. There is no 'soul' trapped in the prison of his twisted body and "peeping out through his eyes", as a sentimental person said on one occasion -indeed his response was once so limited that we never even had eye-contact. Practical reality keeps one's feet on the ground. Even if it were conceivable that someone should wave a magic wand tomorrow, cause his brain to expand to normal size and make it function normally, he would not be 'normal' (whatever that means!): for he has missed out on twenty-five years of learning experience. And if that were miraculously supplied, in what sense would Arthur still be Arthur? If the survival of a soul has any significance, it surely involves personal identity. But Arthur's personal identity is inseparable from his limited brain function.

Now of course, neither of these perceptions of mine has remained unchanged since their initial challenge to once-held naive presuppositions. My reflections on Arthur have developed in various ways which will become apparent at a later stage, and my understanding of historical theology has progressed. As a former Classics student I should have been more suspicious of the supposed Hebraic vs Hellenic contrast from the start - after all, Hellenism was the great humanist tradition which offended the Hebrew nation with its glorification of the naked human body in gymnasium, stadium and sculpture; and most Greeks were not Platonists -indeed, some have argued that Plato's immortalising of the soul was an Oriental borrowing. Indeed, it wasn't long before New Testament scholarship was shaken into recognising cross-cultural complexity, as the work of Hengel (*Judaism and Hellenism*, 2 vols. SCM (1974)) drew attention to the fact that Palestine had been under Hellenistic influence for 300 years by the time of Christ. The contrast was always too starkly drawn. It also failed to examine carefully enough the concepts of 'soul' which were around in both traditions. Some of my own research in Fourth Century Christian treatises has demonstrated the extent to which ancient medical philosophers had reflected on the interaction of soul and body, in such a way that soul virtually becomes the equivalent of the central nervous system, providing the mind, the heart, the life and the motive power of the body, which it permeates throughout. There was no crude 'dichotomy' of the human person, though it may have suited us to suggest there was in order to sharpen up our own critique. The analysis needs to be more sophisticated if it is to represent the history of ideas adequately. Furthermore, it is apparent that in developing Christian thought, the Biblical and philosophical traditions naturally cohered with one another - indeed, my paper on the subject was sub-titled, "a study of the interaction of 'science' and the Bible in some anthropological treatises of the Fourth Century". (*Vigiliae Christianae* xxxvii (1983), pp.110-140). The imperative to unveil the coherence between the sacred text and current models whereby the world is understood, is not some new modern phenomenon. The current 'scientific' model was once the 'soul', and the Bible was read in the light of that model. Rather than pretend the 'real meaning' of the Biblical tradition was, conveniently for us now, not an outmoded science, why don't we simply acknowledge that we inevitably read this ancient text from constantly changing perspectives? Our assumptions about the way the world works are shaped by a different set of scientific models from those which have operated in the past. Given that, in what ways are those assumptions 'transvalued' by the Biblical story? I have five main points, but first a note on that phrase, "the Biblical story".

The Bible is not a collection of papers in a scientific journal, and one of the most important things about reading any text or document is to identify its 'genre', if you read a novel as if it were a biography, or vice versa, you will get the whole thing wrong. We could spend the rest of the weekend discussing the correct genre of the Bible: it is of course an ancient library of texts which themselves belong to a variety of genres. But for the moment, suffice it for me to say this - as an authorised canon the Bible presents an over-arching narrative whose plot and characters are summarised in the creeds. In other words, it presents a narrative which purports to sketch the story of the universe, a universal story into which our stories are drawn, and which invests the whole with sense, purpose and direction. It is at the level of giving meaning to existence that the Bible functions, and it does so in a literary way, rather than a scientific way. The deduction of doctrinal, even quasi-scientific, propositions from the Bible has had an important function in Christian history, but that is far from having been the only, or even the principal, way in which the Bible has functioned in the life of the church. In preaching and spirituality, the character-models and story-lines have been of far greater influence in shaping people's understanding of their lives.

Appreciation of the story-character of Biblical truth should assist our project. We are seeking to discover how this over-arching viewpoint 'transvalues' the assumptions we inevitably make about our human existence, given current scientifically established models.

So to our five points:

1. Reductionism and the priority of God

The consequence of giving up the idea of 'soul' is apparently reductionist.

Human existence is reduced to biochemical processes. It is not just religious believers who have difficulties with this. The claims of morality founder on inexorable natural processes. We may have outgrown the old mechanistic views of the universe, but when schizophrenia is shown to have a physical cause in brain chemistry, the line between genius and madness is even more difficult to draw. Heredity and environment easily become totalising explanations of human behaviour. Human responsibility is reduced, it seems, as with the loss of 'soul', human being becomes purely a set of physical reactions. But there is also theological gain. The notion of an immortal soul gives a human being an 'automatic' eternal being and significance. But that is certainly not the implication of the Biblical story. What is clear in the Bible is the priority of God, not merely temporally but existentially. It is not just that God created in the beginning, but that everything is and remains contingent upon God (cf. the creation Psalm 104; Job 38-41, etc.). Nothing has independent being, and without God's creative intention to sustain, even human persons 'dissolve'. There is no guaranteed, automatic survival. As the book of Ecclesiastes puts it:

> ...the fate of humans and the fate of animals is the same; as one dies, so dies the other. They all have the same breath, and humans have no advantage over the animals; for all is vanity. All go to one place: all are from the dust, and all turn to dust again. Who knows whether the human spirit goes upward and the spirit of animals goes downward to the earth?

(I frequently reflect that it would have been good if people had remembered that text during the Darwinist controversy in the Nineteenth Century!) The Bible insists that we belong to the created order, and that our existence is rooted in the cosmos. Since physicality is essential to the creation, we are embodied, like everything else, and our bodies function like the rest of the created order, including our brains and central nervous system. Like the cosmos, we have being only in relation to the Creator, and with respect to the purpose and intention of the God who gives us being. And that, of course, is the essential point. A theological account of the universe permits us to be realistically reductionist about our creaturely constitution as human beings, while leaving open the possibility that God's purpose and intention might transcend biochemical reactions. Talk of 'soul' or 'spirit' might become not so much a claim to a supposed little spiritual mannikin inside our physical frame, as a way of referring to the gift of divine transcendence, earthed in our physical being. We have a profound hunch that human existence is more significant than the cycle of birth and natural decay. But that significance rests in God. I believe that to be true not just of great saints, but of limited beings like my Arthur, the purpose of whose life it is difficult to articulate in any rational or utilitarian way. Human being is contingent upon God, and upon God's will to give it meaning and significance. Thus the curious doctrine of bodily resurrection is important, despite the Bishop of Durham! The Biblical story is not about some kind of spiritual disembodied continuation - the immortality of the soul - whether we are speaking of Jesus or those adopted into Christ; rather it is about re-creation, God restoring a whole person for a renewed and transformed existence. Of course, neither our experience nor our language can cope with the idea, but Paul does better by speaking of a 'spiritual body' than many of his successors who think spiritual and physical are opposites, and incompatible.

Which brings me to the second point:

2. The physical as medium of the spiritual

The problem with the notion of 'soul' is that it creates a dualism, the human being becomes a composite being, and the fundamental anthropological problem becomes how the (impassible) soul relates to the (passible) body. The body becomes a kind of 'spacesuit' for the soul, which is the 'real person'. For existence in this atmospheric environment, the body provides the necessary life-support systems, but it is also something of an encumbrance. The soul is the source of life and movement, yet it is dangerously dragged down by passions and emotions associated with the flesh. There are passages in Paul's epistles which seem to encourage such a view, but only because they are interpreted through that outdated model. Paul does not seem to look forward to some kind of existence as a naked soul - using mixed metaphorical language, he says:

> "......in this tent we groan, longing to be clothed with our heavenly dwelling - if indeed, when we have taken it off we will not be found naked. For while we are still in this tent, we groan under our burden, because we wish not to be unclothed but to be further clothed, so that what is mortal swallowed up by life." (2 Cor.5:2-4)

The NRSV translation is about as unclear as the original, but Paul certainly wants, not to be naked, but in some sense to be better clothed, and the clothing Paul has in mind is Christ:

> "As many of you as were baptized into Christ have clothed yourselves with Christ" (Gal.3:27)

> "....you have stripped off the old self with its practices and clothed yourselves with the new self, which is being renewed in knowledge according to the image of its creator" (Col.3:9-10).

In fact, the more one ponders Paul, the clearer it seems to be that despite his language, Paul's conception is not of a dualism of spirit and flesh, but rather two spheres or conditions of existence. 'Flesh' stands for the old order, represented by Adam, damaged by sin and disobedience; 'spirit' for the new creation, represented by Christ, humanity renewed by his obedience. This new humanity is God's new creation out of the dust and ashes, as it were, of the old. When Paul insists that God sent

> "his own Son in the likeness of sinful flesh and to deal with sin" (Rom.8:3),

or that

> "For our sake he made him to be sin who knew no sin, so that in him we might become the righteousness of God" (2 Cor.5:21),

what he is asserting is that

> "if anyone is in Christ, there is a new creation: everything old has passed away; see, everything has become new!" (2 Cor.5:17).

And the point is that this is a renewal of the gone-wrong created order, and of the corrupted and diseased human being which is part of it. The incarnation implies that the physical is the medium of God's creative presence and activity:

> "... the creation itself will be set free from its bondage to decay and will obtain the freedom of the glory of the children of God. We know that the whole creation has been groaning in labour pains until now; and not only the creation but we ourselves, who have the first-fruits of the Spirit, groan inwardly awaiting the redemption of our bodies" (Rom. 8:21-3).

The whole heaven and earth, the universe, and our physical human existence hangs together. This Pauline vision of new creation in Christ is set in the over-arching story of the cosmos, a cosmos for which God had intentions which went awry, and which depends for its future and the realisation of its promise on the continued creative and redemptive activity of the divine Spirit. Salvation is not escape from the material world to a spiritual heaven. The spiritual is immanent in the physical, and matter is its medium.

Which brings me naturally to the third main point:

3. The whole is more than the sum of its parts

Scientific interest for a long time sought explanation by finer and finer analysis. The table, it turned out, was not solid after all, but a whirling mass of particles. Biblical study likewise analysed the text into sources, desperate to find the 'original'. Now scholars are recognising that the importance of the analysis is that it permits discernment of the new significance the parts take on when they are integrated into the whole. Intellectual interest has turned to ecology - the question of interlocking, interdependent systems. There are emergent properties which belong to the larger whole but not the 'components' as identified by analysis.

With respect to human nature, Ross Thompson (Holy Ground, SPCK (1990)) puts it like this:

> "The logic of explanation here leads us to considerations of levels. Within a level, a set of categories remains applicable when we try to explain parts of a system by other parts; when we try to explain those categories themselves, we step down a level. In explaining human behaviour we invoke psychological talk of desires, beliefs, thoughts and so forth; to explain those categories we have to step down a level and use the physiological and neurophysiological language of brain and body states, life processes and organ functions. To explain those in turn we invoke electrochemical language of reactions taking place inside cells, and then to explain those we use the physical language of atoms and elementary particles. So a well-recognised conceptual hierarchy is built up."

But

> "If we confuse levels, we make a category mistake. Thus it is neither true nor false but meaningless to speak of an atom as having purpose, or conversely to speak of a human being

> in terms of atomic reactions. I call this 'categorical transcendence'. That which transcends x neither is nor is not-x, it lies beyond the realm to which the concept of x-ness is applicable. We can transcend upwards or downwards in the hierarchy. Thus human life transcends the atomic level, but equally the atom transcends the human level."

Later in the book, the emergence of order and its symbiotic relationship with chaos in what we might call 'shuffling' natural systems enables Ross Thompson to speak of an

> "unknowably deep simplicity that generates the infinite ever-novel complexity of the world around us" (p.203).

Now I am not altogether competent to assess his exposition of scientific and philosophical thinking, but his argument that the "dust is magic" I find very intriguing. One more quotation:

> "The way we are is the outcome of an evolution prefigured even in the primal dust, in which ever more intricate games have been played out with the elementary forces and tested for fecundity. The wing of a bird embodies one skill of matter relating to matter - the forces of life engaging with the forces of air - and in that skill there is embedded a kind of knowing, albeit tacit. The human brain and hands and artefacts and voice embody other diousiae, other attunements of matter to matter, skills of explicitly knowing that extend to the farthest horizon of the universe; so that in these human things that are part of the universe, the universe comes to know itself. Often such thoughts are taken somehow to demean thought and the human; but we do not demean a string quartet by pointing out that it is played on bits of cat-gut......."

Thompson's whole argument is summed up in his sub-title, The

Spirituality of Matter. I have myself pointed out on earlier occasions the fact that music is impossible without its 'incarnation' in the physical realities of vibrating strings, air-waves in tubes, ear-drums which function, etc., and yet we know that it cannot be reduced to that. The spiritual 'emerges' in the physical integration of material things. The whole is greater than the sum of its parts.

In a sense, this third point is a kind of exegesis of the second in terms that have some hope of making sense in relation to current scientific and philosophical thinking. It is because it reaches the same fundamental conclusion, that the relationship between the 'transcendent' or emergent 'spiritual' level to the physical or material is not a dualistic one, that it can be regarded as essentially biblical. In fact, the first three points cohere with the over-arching biblical story of a physical universe contingent upon God, its Creator.

But the Biblical story suggests that we may be able to go further. Clearly an emergent spiritual level characterises human being as an individual organism greater than the whole of its biochemical parts. But suppose there is an even more advanced spiritual level that emerges in the Body of Christ. Human social organisation, group dynamics, etc., can of course also be treated as producing a 'level' beyond its individual components.

As in the case of the individual, so also this level, according to Paul and the Biblical tradition, has a propensity to 'go wrong' -generating structures of evil and violence. Corporate humanity, like the individual, may well belong to the old Adam. But the Biblical story is of the creation of a new corporate humanity, belonging to a second, or heavenly, Adam. "In Christ we are a new creation" is far from being individualistic in Paul's thinking. It is in community that the fruits of the Spirit emerge: love, joy, peace, patience, kindness, generosity, faithfulness, gentleness and self-control - these qualities cannot be exercised, these values pursued, in splendid isolation. They belong to community.

The Biblical story speaks of humanity as the crown of God's creation, made in God's image. It then speaks of this creation missing its mark, falling short of the glory of God. Then again it speaks of Christ as the image of God, restoring the creation to its fullness of being. That new image of God is curiously more than an individual - the Body of Christ is a community, an emergent spiritual whole greater than its parts. Even my Arthur belongs to that transcendent reality. The fruits of the Spirit are values that include the weak and vulnerable in such a way that apparent non-contributors become indispensable to the whole, which is considerably more significant than any individual parts.

4. 'Cosmic' significance

What I have said so far has frequently drawn attention to the 'cosmic' dimension of the Biblical story, and the importance of human beings having a realistic grasp on their place in the universe. I would argue that within Christian tradition there was a far better grasp of the kind of truths I've been outlining prior to the advent of modernity. One aspect of postmodernity is a little more willingness to see the value of classic ideas - at least in architecture if not so obviously in other spheres. So let me take you back to the fourth century, and some of the Christianised wisdom of the ancients which shaped the mediaeval world.

A commonplace in antiquity was that the macrocosm is imaged in the microcosm - that is, the whole universe can be seen in humanity, and humanity reflects or images the whole universe. The human person was seen as the integration of material and spiritual components, soul and body. The universe likewise was composed of spiritual and material. As the 'soul' permeated the body and gave it life, and without it the body dies and disintegrates, so the universe was permeated by the divine Spirit. Already in the book known as the Wisdom of Solomon we can see such notions expressed within the Judaeo-Christian tradition, though they originated in the philosophy of Aristotle and the Stoics:

> "(In wisdom) there is ... a spirit that is intelligent, holy, unique, manifold, subtle, mobile, clear unpolluted, distinct,

> invulnerable, loving the good, keen, irresistible, beneficent, humane, steadfast, sure, free from anxiety, all-powerful, overseeing all, and penetrating through all spirits that are intelligent, pure, and altogether subtle. For wisdom is more mobile than any motion; because of her pureness she pervades and penetrates all things. For she is the breath of the power of God, and a pure emanation of the glory of the Almighty; therefore nothing defiled gains entrance into her. For she is a reflection of eternal light, a spotless mirror of the working of God, and an image of his goodness. Although she is but one, she can do all things, and while remaining in herself, she renews all things; in every generation she passes into holy souls and makes them friends of God and prophets; for God loves nothing so much as the person who lives with wisdom. She is more beautiful than the sun, and excels every constellation of the stars. Compared with the light she is found to be superior, for it is succeeded by the night, but against wisdom evil does not prevail. She reaches mightily from one end of the earth to the other, and she orders all things well..."

Would I could go on with the quotation, but in this life we all operate with constraints, and time presses! This conception of Wisdom was deeply influential in early Christianity, and I want to highlight three ideas:

(1.) Because creation happened through God's Wisdom, this spirit pervading the whole universe was a way of speaking of God's immanence, and of linking the immanence of God's order, goodness and beauty in the universe as a whole with the immanence of God's intelligence, goodness and love in human beings. This cosmic wisdom was identified with the Logos -the Word or Reason that Stoicism identified as the immanent divine in all things, and as the rationality immanent in human being. This identification enabled its association with the Word of God in scripture, the Word by which God created (in Genesis, God spoke and things came into being), the Word by which God spoke through the prophets, the Word which was incarnate in Jesus Christ.

So although the language sounds as if they were speaking of a discrete sort of matter slipping through the interstices of physical being, or a kind of spiritual ether which no-one has been able to find and identify, it is more like the non-physical entity 'mind'.

I am told by the Professor of Computer Science that there is a very mysterious relationship between software and hardware in a computer - no straight -forward correlation exists between my word-processing activities and the physical effects produced thereby in chips making up the machine. He would argue that 'mind' relates to 'brain' in a similarly mysterious way. Ancient philosophers were struggling when it came to conceiving of incorporeal or immaterial entities: Stoics tended to abandon the project and settle for a discrete ether-like matter; Platonists on the contrary considered 'mind' and non-physical entities, like God and the soul, to be superior to all forms of matter. In the light of our discussion, perhaps we should cease to see these as the only alternatives: the Spirit pervades everything as 'mind' relates to brain, software to hardware.

Now if that analogy has some kind of meaning, then the ancient notion that there is an underlying unity in the way the universe works and the way a human being works perhaps has some renewed vitality. They saw both human being and the cosmos as a composite unity of physical and spiritual. We can short-circuit the dualism, and see parallel 'levels' in cosmos and humankind, levels at which we have to begin to talk of the whole as being incarnated or embodied intelligence, more than the sum of its parts. (This is not all that far from the project of Process Theologians. My reservation with respect to their approach would be that it properly applies to exploring the relationship of the immanent Spirit to the created order, and the Biblical story demands that God be also the transcendent other. Now is not the time to get distracted in Trinitarian theology, but I am sure it is indispensable.)

So to sum up, one might say, the cosmos, the community, the person is potentially a Temple of the divine Spirit, not in the sense of housing something other, but in the sense that a Temple ceases to be a Temple if it is reduced to the mere materials from which it is built and the indwelling Spirit is not taken to be constitutive of its being a Temple.

(2.) The New Testament picks up aspects of this picture of Wisdom in developing its Christology. Thus the Epistle to the Hebrews echoes this language when it describes the Son of God as

> "the reflection of God's glory and the exact imprint of God's very being."

The Prologue of John's Gospel uses the term Logos -Word -rather than Wisdom, but certainly sees this cosmic Reason as embodied in Jesus Christ in a particular way. There used to be much talk in theological circles about the 'scandal of particularity', but it seems to me that here lies the genius of Christianity. Particulars are significant precisely because they instance universals, and yet have their own particular identity. To be pregnant is to go through one of the most significant and particular personal experiences; but when you go to the clinic, you find you are one among hundreds. As with birth, so with death. And so too Jesus Christ.

Jesus belongs to the particularities of unrepeatable history, and yet has cosmic, universal significance. Why? Because in Christ the cosmic Wisdom of God was present renewing all things according to God's original purpose and intention. Human beings become cosmically significant as they are caught up in that process.

(3.) This Wisdom-idea became identified with the Holy Spirit. So how do we distinguish the cosmic Christ and the cosmic Spirit? I guess there has been confusion in Christian theology down the centuries. Perhaps in terms of the understanding we are developing here, we could suggest that both instance God's immanence and presence in the cosmos, but in different ways. The Spirit pervades macrocosm and microcosm, whereas the incarnate Christ instances the divine purpose for human being as the image of God. Both provide a vision of creation's potential, actualising that spiritual element which so often fails to emerge from our physical existence.

My final point serves also as conclusion:

5. The Temple of the Holy Spirit

In speaking of creation's potential we may well fall into the same old trap as the old notion of the immortal soul - namely imagining an inbuilt natural process. Both positions may, of course, be partially redeemed by referring to the fact that God the Creator built it in. But the importance of our being embodied, being physically constrained, vulnerable and mortal creatures, is precisely to keep our feet on the ground. As the great tragic literature of the world keeps exploring, human greatness lies at the margins, in the struggle with the constraints of existence, and when someone over-reaches themselves, claiming immortality, absolute power, divinity, then power corrupts, greatness becomes sin, humanity falls and great is the fall thereof.

Yet that is not the whole of the story, whether we speak of humanity or the universe. The story is that the whole is in relationship with God, who constantly seeks to bring good out of evil, order out of chaos, creatively engaging with the world which is entirely contingent upon God and the divine will that things should exist and remain in existence, should exist physically in such a way that the physical becomes the medium which permits the emergence of the spiritual.

As individuals, then, we claim the promise that our bodies may be Temples of the Holy Spirit. As Christian communities, we claim the promise that we, the Body of Christ, may be indwelt by God's Spirit, so becoming a truer Temple than any building. And even as we recognise the Spirit of God presently at work in the cosmos, we look for the renewal of the whole, the resurrection of the dead and the life of the world to come, the realisation of God's wise intention in the new heaven and earth, where the seer saw no temple,

> "for its temple is the Lord God the Almighty and the Lamb. And the city has no need of sun or moon to shine on it, for the glory of God is its light, and its lamp is the Lamb .... (and) People will bring into it the glory and the honour of the nations" (Rev.21:22-6).

QUESTIONS following Professor Young's Lecture

Q. **It is said that modern people no longer fear death because they do not believe in an after life, but that they do fear oblivion. Many believe that human life has no meaning and that it just disappears into the dustbin of history. Would you comment on that?**

A. I think the difficulties arise for us because of our long tradition, perhaps particularly in the evangelical tradition, of demanding a conscious response to the gospel as the way of salvation. It seems to me in pondering on the parables of Jesus that Jesus is often saying that you religious people who think that you have got the answers are in fact the ones who are going to get there last. It is the human beings who instinctively know what is good and right, whether they believe in God or not and whether they respond to Jesus Christ or not, who perhaps have it more right than those of us who are consciously claiming to have it right. I think that actually is a very important point. Jesus said, 'Judge not, that ye be not judged.'

My own response to a deepening sense of the priority of God is that we have to leave the ultimate destiny of the universe and all humanity in God's hands, and trust. It is, of course, good Methodist tradition that God will ultimately save everybody. But it is also good Methodist tradition that people can freely reject. There is a tension there. We have to leave open the possibility that God honours the dignity and freedom of everybody to the point of allowing people to dissolve into nothingness, if that is the way they have chosen to go. But these are extremely complex and difficult questions, and there are points where an agnostic position is better than anything else.

One thing this means is that the concept of heaven and hell as some other place to which we may or may not go, is fairly problematic in relation to our understanding of the universe as it is emerging. One of the things which is in my lecture and which arises out of the biblical material is the notion that the new creation, the restoration of a new heaven and a new earth, which is what Revelation is all about, is actually the goal of the present existence. However hard it is to conceive, that is actually an honouring of the dignity of our physical reality, and is much more likely to be the kind of goal which God intends to move towards than this world simply being a dead end and heaven and hell being the aim.

What is important is that we should regain a sense of transcendence. Twentieth century Christianity has become so earthed in the here and now that there is a sense in which Christians hope and Christian recognition of the fact that this world is not the way God intends has tended to get a bit lost. We need to realise that.

Q. **Your lecture was extremely clear on immanence, especially the immanence of the Spirit. There is a theory that, in this 'many levels' account that you gave, the material universe is itself creating the level above, and so on for successive levels. So I wonder if you would comment on the concept of God as 'other'.**

A. I do not think that the otherness of God is important. This theory to which you refer could be seen to be somewhat similar to that of process theologians, some of whom more or less said that the universe is God's body. In other words, they have taken the microcosm/macrocosm thing almost more literally that I have. They talk about God developing and changing as the universe develops and changes. This is obviously quite a considerable challenge to long-standing traditions about the nature of

God. Some of that is interesting in relation to the notion of the immanence of the Spirit within the cosmos, which is what I have been mainly talking about. But it is also important that we maintain the long tradition of God not being an object like other objects in the universe. The trouble is as we objectify God like that and wrap our minds around God, we reduce God and he becomes some sort of superman. I'm enough of a feminist to object to a superman!

One of the essential things in the tradition particularly of Eastern Orthodoxy is what is called the apophatic tradition of theology, which means that you can only say what God is not; you can't say what God is. For example, God is incorporeal, that is, non-bodily and non-physical. Or God is invisible, not visible. And so on through a whole string of negatives. The only thing you can say about the being of God is a negation of what we know in this world is a very important theological tradition. I suspect that we need to hold onto that for all kinds of reasons. That is one of the reasons why I said that Trinitarian theology is very important. This too is very deep within the Eastern Orthodox tradition. Of course, it is difficult. It takes a lot of thought to wrap one's mind around it. But it is one of the ways of trying to speak of God as both transcendent, that is, other than the world, and also immanent.

One image I like from early Christian theology is of the Word and of the Spirit being the two hands of God. The hands are the instruments through which a human being creates, and it is through the Word and the Spirit that God creates. So God, who is totally other and unknown in his being, is known to us through the divine activities which we know through the Word and the Spirit. That too is a very important tradition in the Eastern Orthodoxy. We cannot know God in his essential being. Because we are finite and God is infinite, there is no way we can get our minds wrapped around God and contain God. In fact, God is the one who contains everything. We only know God through the divine activities in creation and revelation. I want to maintain that that kind of complex but difficult theological position is essential to our understanding.

Q. **I have always believed that resurrecting or not resurrecting is God's activity. We do not raise ourselves. How can one cope in a pastoral capacity in bereavements where one feels that the deceased was very far from being a saint deserving to be raised?**

A. I would simply take you back to the quotation I gave earlier from the Sermon on the Mount, "Judge not, that ye be not judged." We do have to say that there are very few human beings who do not have some glimmering of those values which we see to be at the heart of God's universe. When one is affirming the life of someone at the moment of death in the midst of their loved ones, it is clearly important to affirm and to assert that God values what value there is there. Secondly, even when you are burying a saint, it is quite a good idea to remember that we are all sinners and we all fall short of the glory of God. There but for the grace of God we all go. My starting point in theology is increasingly that we have to start with 'God is God is God'. There has been far too much assumption that we know and we determine who is in and who is out. Before that Reality we must remember in humility our creatureliness, and the possibility that many of us might just simply dissolve like all other created things do, dissolving and giving new life. It is an amazing thing to go into a piece of virgin forest and see the nurse logs. As the trees die, they become the nurse of the new trees. That sense of the cycle of death and birth within natural processes is a very intriguing parable.

Maybe that is the fundamental thing we need to hold on to, that God is always bringing new life out of death, however hard it is for us to understand. The traditional mythology of heaven and hell is not adequate, and if that is so, then purgatory doesn't fit either. However, one can't necessarily rule out that God's long-term intention is a continuing, on-going, creative process. Therefore those who, to put it crudely, 'don't make the grade when they die', may find other ways in which the process goes on. We have to think through what the old mythologies were getting at, rather than take them in too literal a fashion.

Q. **Are we in the Christian tradition ignoring an enormous wisdom about the cosmos which might be found in other religious traditions?**

A. Yes, there are things in all cultures and traditions of the world that can be instructive and can illuminate our own. I suspect, however, that if we look deep enough, there are similar traditions within our particular Christian culture.

It's not quite sure, however, whether you are asking me to affirm an openness to truth wherever we find it, which I would certainly affirm. I would say in a sense the early Christian Logos doctrine was affirming just that. In the second century Christians were even affirming that Socrates had the Logos. In other words, the Logos or Reason, which is the divine reason at the heart of everything, is in all truth wherever it comes from. But they would go on to say that this was fully seen in Jesus Christ, and therefore Jesus Christ gives the criterion for understanding where truth is. The Logos theology is very important in the early Church and has a lot to teach us now about this whole area of the exclusive and the inclusive within the Christian tradition.

Or were you asking me to comment on particularity? One element in my lecture was a little stress on the importance of particularity. Human minds tend to look for the universal and for the over-arching principles. In the process you evacuate what is actually the truth of our day-to-day existence, which is that we are all particular and we are are particularly different. That particularity is actually an essential part of the universe. There are no two blades of grass which are identical. This is something also which we need to reflect on and think about very carefully. There is a sense in which you can say that God honours the particular and wishes to be in relationship with the particulars which the universe has produced.

Now, it seems to me that a lot of Eastern wisdom is evacuating the particular. You meditate until you become part of the cosmic whole and you cease to value particularity. One of the fundamental differences between the essentially Christian mystical tradition and mystical traditions elsewhere is that theologically Christian mysticism does not claim absorption into the divine. It is always relationship with the divine, which means that the particular being is being honoured rather than absorbed or dissolved into some bigger whole. That is one of the geniuses at the heart of Christianity which we should actually take very seriously as perhaps one of the particular things Christianity has to offer to any kind of global dialogue.

Q. **Would you like to comment on the relationship between atheism and Christian belief?**

A. In Western European tradition the particular kind of theism which has been set forth as the philosophical undergirding of Christianity has been very unfortunate, because it looks like a man blown up big. We use the words 'omnipotent' and 'omnipresent' of God so that the picture is of a God who somehow is like a huge human mind, a picture which has then become quite simply not believable. It does seem to me that the atheist critique has got some very telling points against the tradition of Western theism. I suspect that if Western Christianity had held on much more firmly to the traditions of Eastern Christianity the apophatic and agnostic traditions, the notion that human beings dare not make God in their own image -then that would have actually changed the discussion as it has gone in recent European intellectual history. I think there is a similarity between Christianity and atheism. You might not know that Christians were called atheists in the ancient world. That is quite instructive. Christians were protesting against idolatry, the particular sorts of religion that were around, and they were called atheists because of their nonconformity with the religion of the ancient world. We must recognise the strength of the atheist critique, and see that there has always been this kind of dialectic within the Christian tradition.

Q. **Would you like to comment further on the place, the use, and the way we should treat animals?**

A. We are a kind of animal, we are continuous with the creation, and in general terms Darwin was absolutely right. If only they had remembered that quotation from Ecclesiates in the 19th century, we might have been saved a lot of heartache. Now, what does the Bible say about our relationship with animals? This is becoming an increasingly important issue in Biblical studies. If you look at Genesis, you will find that that phrase which is translated 'have dominion over' doesn't really give the right impression. What you have to remember is that these texts come from nomadic people, and that particular phrase is about being a shepherd. It is not 'having dominion over' in the sense of 'mastery over', which is, of course, what has happened in the last two or three hundred years. It is much more 'having charge of' the creation as a shepherd, as one who collaborates with creation.

Of course, nomadic peoples got their principal sustenance from their flocks and herds. So, from time to time, one of the animals which they were to tend and care for had to become part of their food. But then what you find is that the whole process of slaughtering the animal was a communal rite of sacrifice in which the animal is treated as sacred. No slaughter ever took place except in the context of a religious rite in the early part of the Bible. There is provision for the secular slaughter only after the Jerusalem temple is made the only place where sacrifice could legally take place. So there are ways in which people in our present context are being obliged to go back and look carefully at what the Biblical material is saying. It has appeared to justify exploitation in a most unfortunate way, though I suspect that, when you get down to it, it doesn't really justify exploitation at all.

Q. **You have talked in terms of emerging properties and of various levels of organisation. We have also thought earlier in the Conference of the way in which human personhood could exist in an abstract form as the pattern of neurones independent of the neurones themselves. That still leaves a problem, for that pattern still needs some kind of physical record to recreate the neurone. Would you like to comment on that problem?**

A. We know of no disembodied existence. In fact, even conceiving of disembodied existence is much more difficult than people have imagined. This embodied created order is the only thing we really do know. Impossible though it is to conceive of what the transcendent God might be, there is a sense in which what we know of God is deeply embedded in the physical order. Similarly, our own spiritual level is embodied in the physical order, which is again why think the analogy with music is very good. There is no music until somebody starts hitting the piano keys or drawing a piece of catgut across a string. Until there are sound waves which involve air vibrating and eardrums vibrating in response, there is no music. It is inseparable from its physical reality, and yet most of us who enjoy music would say that you can't reduce it simply to the physical reality. That is the conundrum I was trying to explore without being a scientist.

Q. **What is your opinion of near-death experiences, or of those experiences in which people claim to have looked down on themselves in an operating theatre or in some other situation?**

A. Along with many other people who work in brain science, I can probably find some reductionist explanation. You only have to think of what happens in dreams, and then you have the interesting question what does happen in dreams? Is it just all sorts of firing of bits of memory chasing around in your head without much rational control? or do dreams have a greater significance, either psychologically like Freud thought, or religiously like the Bible thinks? It is very hard indeed to come up with a solution to those questions which everybody will embrace. I have no doubt there are plenty of people who would see these sorts of experiences as simply some kind of brain activity.

As for making anything else of it, there is always a difficulty in assessing subjective experience. The same is true of claims to religious experience of any kind. If I say I was called to the ministry when it seemed as though a voice spoke at some traffic lights at Dudley, I cannot convince another person that it was a real event. Indeed, I find it sometimes quite difficult to convince myself, because there is a sense in which it was my interpretation of a thought that went through my mind in terms of the biblical narratives that have shaped my understanding of the world since I was a very small person.

So it does seem to me that there is a variety of different ways in which people would seek to give explanations of those sorts of things. What I would want to say is that the spiritual, the communication of God with those who live on the earth, is always necessarily through the physical make-up and culture of those who are at the receiving end of the communication. You can't get away from that. That is true of the Bible too. The theological principle which you find in the early church is that God accommodates the divine self to the human level. You can say that of the incarnation and of the word of scripture. If God is communicating with a group of people whose language is Hebrew, he has to communicate in Hebrew.

Of course, the question then is, how do you distinguish God's communication from any other kind of communication? You can't give any knock-down proof. But what I would want to say about all claims to religious experience, and to the kind of experiences referred to in the question, is that we cannot judge from outside what is happening, because they are subjective experiences. In the Bible we are told that you have to test the spirits, and one of the ways in which the spirits are to be tested is by their fruits. The fruits of the Spirit are love, joy, peace, patience and so on. It is actually important not simply to accept every claim to religious experience. It has to be considered in relation to the values which it produces. There was, after all, the bloke who went off and carried a whole lot of people with him, and settled in a community somewhere in Latin America, and then they all committed suicide together. Was that genuine religious experience? Similarly with the recent tragedy in Waco.

It does seem to me that, when you get into the complex area of religious experience, it is very hard indeed to know what to make of it. That problem has been there right from the start. How did Jeremiah prove that he was a true prophet when there were all those false prophets around? All the people thought that the false prophets were much more likely to be right than Jeremiah. That is probably not a very direct answer to the question, but I hope that you can see the context.

Comment from the floor: From a purely medical point of view, these people haven't died, because they are back here to tell us about it. What they have experienced is becoming unconscious through hypoxic brain failure. People who go further than that, and resuscitate, may come back with severe brain damage; or they may go beyond that, not be resuscitated at all, and die. It is rather like being anaesthetised and experiencing going to sleep. Maybe it tells you that is what you would experience if you died that way. Maybe it tells you that dying that way is not unpleasant. But by definition they have not died, because the brain is still working.

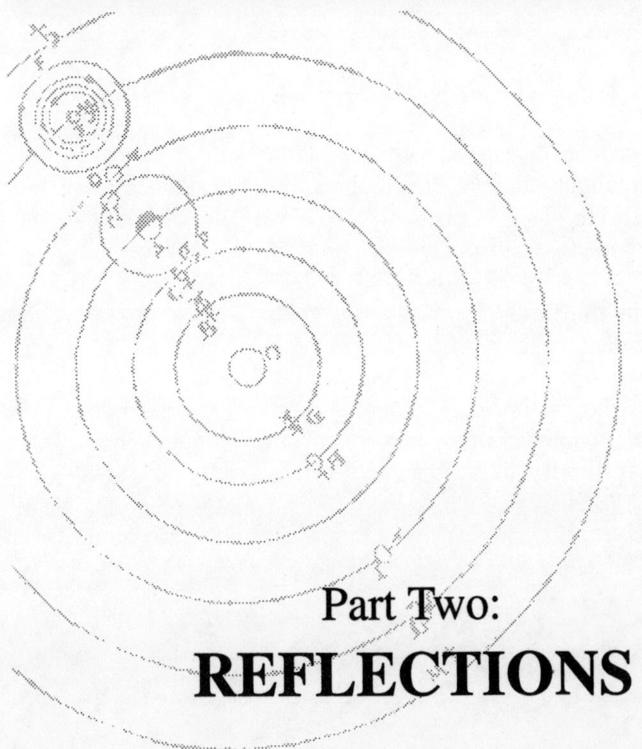

Part Two:
REFLECTIONS

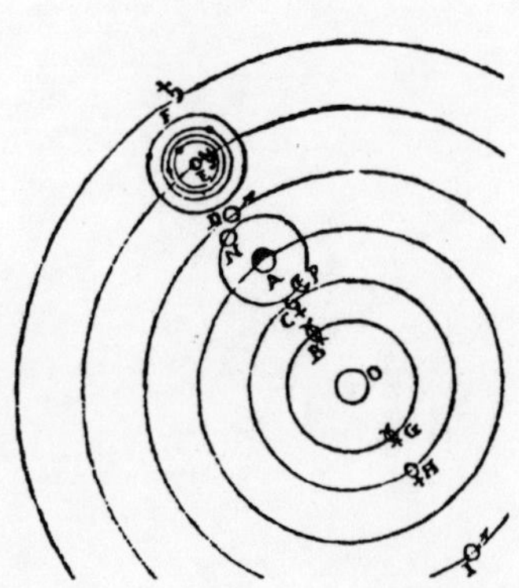

Sermon

Rev. David Winter

It's a privilege to be asked to preach at your service this morning and fascinating to preach at a conference with this particular title.

Let me start with my text:

> "As you sent me into the world, I have sent them into the world" (John 17:18).

The "world" is cosmos in both cases. Cosmos is an intriguing word. Christ and the Cosmos. I looked it up in the Oxford Dictionary, which is always a rewarding thing for a preacher to do, because I was intrigued to think what you were actually engaged in. That defines cosmos as 'the universe as a well-ordered whole'. I could see from things which had been said about this conference that would be the sort of thinking, or part of the thinking, that lay behind it. But I also knew, and half an hour with the Greek dictionary proved the fact, that in Greek it means a few more things as well. And so I want to give, if I may, a short survey of the New Testament cosmos and some of the marks that it gives us of the truth of God.

In Greek in New Testament times cosmos firstly meant 'order'. Secondly, it can be used for 'beauty' or adornment - hence 'cosmetic'. Then it can mean the material universe, the aggregate of created existence, the earth, and once or twice mankind. And finally, and most commonly in the New Testament, it meant the present order of things, the secular world, society organised without reference to God. Now, actually Christ relates to all of these definitions. I just want to look at those different meanings of cosmos in the New Testament.

First of all, what are the marks of the cosmos that the New Testament use of 'cosmos' gives us? Think first of the beginnings of the fourth Gospel - and, incidentally, it is the fourth Gospel and the first letter of John in which the word cosmos appears most often. John 1:10,

> "The world was made through him."

I think that offers the first mark of the cosmos in the New Testament. It is created, not made and not self-existent. The distinction between creator and maker is slight but important. Once upon a time these pews were a tree somewhere, and then with the involvement of some glue and nails and the skill of the carpenter were turned into seats. They were something else and they became seats, and you can probably say that somebody was their maker. But that person wasn't their creator. The maker takes something that already exists and reshapes it. God is the creator in the sense that Beethoven created his 7th Symphony. That is to say, before the first note was written it didn't exist, and then from within Beethoven and entirely from him the 7th Symphony came into being. It was created by Beethoven in the sense that it owes everything to him, and wouldn't have existed without him. The universe is created in that sense. It comes from God, it wouldn't exist without him, it is entirely of his devising.

Secondly, the cosmos is orderly, the root of the word itself. It's a universe of order. I gather that is the thing that attracts most scientists to the study of it. The same rules apply at the limits of the universe when we explore it as we do on our own doorstep.

Thirdly, it is beautiful. Paul says in Romans that we are without excuse if we don't believe in God, having seen his universe, presumably having seen its order and its beauty. The Psalms are full of this idea.

> "In beauty you have made them all".

> "The earth is full of your glory."

Creation, the universe, the cosmos, is beautiful.

And fourthly, it is purposeful. It is not an accident and it is not a nonsense. It has a purpose:

> "The heavens declare the glory of God".

It speaks of a creator who has a purpose for it. We look for a new heaven and a new earth in which dwell righteousness. Things are not accidental, but purposeful.

Those seem to me the marks of the cosmos in terms of the universe, the created order. But what are the marks of the cosmos in that other meaning -the present order of things? That is the sense in which cosmos is used endlessly in the fourth Gospel and in John's first letter:

"Love not the world nor the things of the world".

I think the marks of the present order of things, both in Bible times and today, are usually the same. They are perhaps more marked today because we are more open about them. The marks of the present order of things, that is to say, the secular world, society organised without reference to God, are a denial of creation and the enthronement of Man. For if there is no God, then I am my God and my wishes are sovereign. The denial of creation is a difficult and dangerous road to go down because if there is no creator I may presumably please myself.

The second mark of the present order of things would be a breakdown of order. I don't mean law and order, though I suppose that comes into it, but fragmentation of society and of art; perhaps you can always see these things mirrored most in art. There was a time when plays were written within a classical formula. They had to take place within a certain period of time, within a certain location. They had a thesis and antithesis, we might say a beginning, a middle and an end. In much modern art and writing no such form exists, no such order. Fragmentation is the object and nothing is the end. How many times in the 60s and 70s did you watch the Wednesday play on BBC Tv, and just when it was getting interesting and you thought it might be going to give you an answer, the credits began to roll, because the dramatist had actually said, "There is no answer, there is no sense, existence is literally nonsense and that is what we are showing you"? Jesus said,

"He who does not gather with me scatters".

This fragmentation of society is something of which many of us are aware, and I believe it springs fundamentally from the present order of things, society organised as if God does not exist.

Following on from that comes a rejection of purpose, that is to say, existentialism, the theatre of the absurd. Because there is no purpose in the cosmos, then all choices are equally valid and my opinion is as good as yours, and the direction in which I want things to go is as valid as yours. It is quite a new idea really and it gets deeply into modern thinking. Many people live purposeless lives and would say so. I've talked to many people in business, in the arts and in the communications world who find their only validity in their work (or sometimes in their personal relationships), and can see no other greater purpose in life at all. No wonder they are demoralised by retirement or redundancy or by the breakdown of human relationships.

And the fourth mark of the cosmos as the present order of things would be for me a flight from beauty into the cult of ugliness. Again this has happened in past ages, but more notably so in the post - war era and today, the elevation of ugliness to an art form, not just in music and art, but in clothing, in language, in what we might call in an old - fashioned word 'manner'. This is the glorification of the ugly, as though we can argue against the creation by taking a little bit of it and turning it from its natural beauty into an unnatural disorder and ugliness. No wonder Jesus says about his disciples in his prayer in John 17,

> "the world has hated them".

For they are bearers of the word. Now, that word is the word of order, purpose and beauty of the one "through whom all things were made". The bearers of the word testify to a cosmos of order, purpose, beauty and truth. And the world -this definition of it, this present order of things, society organised as though God did not exist -hates that because it is totally contrary to where it stands.

What are the marks of the redemption of the cosmos? Now, that seems to be the theme that has run through a lot that we have already heard this morning. It comes back to my text:

> "As you sent me into the world, I send them into the world",

echoed again in the fourth Gospel after the resurrection,

> "as the father sent me, so send I you".

This is John 3:16 -

> "God so loved the cosmos that he gave his only Son".

Now, what is this cosmos that God loves? Why, in the fourth Gospel it is entirely society organised as though he does not exist. The God-rejecting, Christ-crucifying world is the world that God loves. Now, we are told not to love the world or the things of the world. That is to say, we are not to love the world in the sense of aping its manners, conforming ourselves to its way of thinking, and compromising God's order, truth and beauty in order to be acceptable to the current fashion. We are not called to love the world that way. But we are called in Christ to love the world the way God loves it, to love it to redemption. John 3:17 is not so often quoted:

> "God did not send his son into the cosmos to condemn the cosmos, but that the cosmos through him might be saved."

God's purpose is the redemption of the cosmos; not its condemnation but its salvation. So Christ came to seek and to save what was lost. For that cosmos God sent his Son. And now in the name of his Son he sends his Son's followers with the same mission, the redemption of the cosmos, to call the cosmos back to its creator, back to order, back to beauty, back to purpose, to bear reliable witness to those things in a disordered, unbelieving, uncreated, ugly and purposeless world, or a world which is beginning to deify those negative qualities.

The cosmos is loved, the cosmos has been visited and redeemed. And it is now to be infiltrated by agents of the Word, a Word of beauty, truth and purpose, a word not of judgement but of infinite love. May God give us grace to be agents of that marvellous purpose.

A Hymn

Mr Peter Haskins

(based on Psalms 19 and Psalm 8)

Suggested Tune: 'Thaxted' by Holst
(Methodist Hymn Book (1933) No. 900)

Every night when stars are shining
They fill the skies above
And they tell the Father's wisdom,
His glory and his love.
No one's ear can hear them speaking
In the silence of the night,
For the galaxies and stars
Sing melodies of light.
In accord the shining starry skies
In harmony proclaim
All the skill of our Creator's work;
His great and mighty name!

When we look in awe and wonder
And try to understand
Meaning in the spacious universe
Created by His hand;
What are we, His mortal children?
What are we, frail humankind?
Mighty questions deep and awesome
Confound the human mind!
Yet although within the universe
We're humble and so small,
Lovingly, he placed into our hands
Dominion over all!

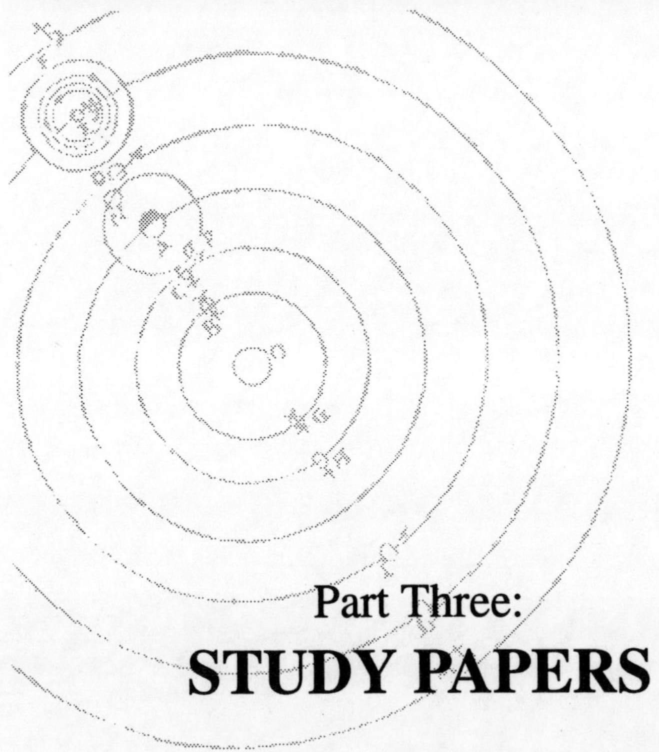

Part Three:

STUDY PAPERS

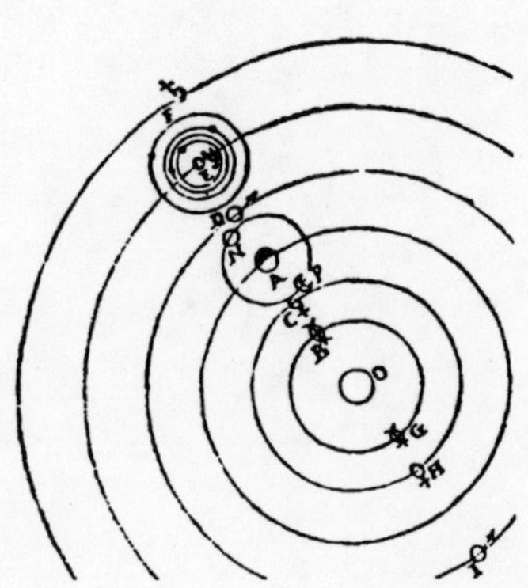

Talking Theology

A Conversation with Rev. Dr. Richard G. Jones

The Rev. Dr. Richard G. Jones, D.D., M.A., B.D. read mechanical sciences at Cambridge and then spent two years in the Royal Navy as a school master, before candidating for the Methodist Ministry. He trained at Hartley Victoria College in Manchester, then served on SCM staff for two years. After serving in two Circuits in Sheffield and one in Birkenhead, he returned to Hartley Victoria college in 1969 as a member of Staff, and subsequently became Principal. He served for one further year in Circuit at Holt in Norfolk, then became Chairman of the East Anglia District of the Methodist Church in 1983. He was President of the Methodist Conference in 1989. Among his publications are **Groundwork of Worship and Preaching** and **Groundwork of Christian Ethics**. His main academic interest is in theology and ethics.

SWR: *There are three broad areas I should like us to talk about, all in the context of our living in a scientific culture and particularly of our being part of a group of science and religion explorers. One area is the Bible, another is human life, but I think the first must necessarily be that of God himself. After all, if God doesn't exist, then the whole of our theology is bunkum and our churchmanship is surely a house of cards which not only could collapse but ought to collapse. So my first question is about the traditional proofs for the existence of God. What are they? are any of them still at all convincing? has anyone come up with any better ones? and, if you are going to tell me that 'proof' is the wrong word, wouldn't it be better to throw in the towel straight away in the science/religion debate?*

RGJ: Well, I am going to suggest that 'proof' isn't a very satisfactory word, though that doesn't mean that we've finished with the science and religion debate. Classically, the so-called proofs for the existence of God were really only reasonable inferences that show that belief in God is tenable and is not daft. That is what they were designed to do. They were also designed to make sense of our experience. For example, the moral experience. Where do we get the notion that some things are right and that we are answerable to 'the right'? I don't think that any philosopher of religion today would want to call them 'proofs', and, even when they were presented as proofs, that wasn't a very satisfactory term.

But there are still today very cogent reasons for believing that belief in God helps us make better sense of all reality and our experience than not believing. That's where many of these traditional approaches are still helpful. It is interesting, for example, that many modern scientists now talk about the Anthropic Principle. What they mean is, why is the universe such that human beings have come about on it, when the chances against that happening are something like 10 to the power 86? Despite those extraordinary odds, nevertheless human beings have come about. And, of course, both scientists and theologians say that is fairly strong evidence that there is a purpose in the universe and that human beings are part of it. That doesn't prove God, but it does show that to believe in a purpose in the universe makes more sense than not doing so.

SWR: *Would you think that the Anthropic Principle could be regarded as an up-date of the Cosmological Argument?*

RGJ: Yes, it is one of the modern versions of it really.

SWR: *And the Teleological and the Ontological arguments? Do they still have any force?*

RGJ: Yes, let's put it like this. Modern science as well as religious faith does assume that reality is in the end coherent. It operates in certain fairly structured ways. It is not fundamentally absurd or chaotic. There is sense built in the whole thing. Science has to make that assumption, otherwise it couldn't proceed. If you make it, then you can begin to make sense of the universe. That is a colossal assumption to make, but it is the same sort of assumption as religious people make when they say there is a God who gives meaning and coherence to the whole of the universe. It's like saying that reality is in the end sensible. Now, I think that is the way the modern Ontological Argument actually goes. So if somebody says to us,"What do you mean by God?" we begin in the belief that reality is coherent and that the human mind can begin reasonably to explore it.

SWR: *It might be possible to argue that the fact that the idea of God crops up apparently independently in so many varied cultures is a pointer towards his existence -or at least to a human need to believe in his existence. But, on the other hand, the fact that the various religions present different descriptions of God might point in exactly the other way. So what is God really like? In scientific terms, there seems to be no way of testing the various possibilities. So why should our description of him (or her or it) be more accurate than that of anyone else?*

RGJ: Only if in the end it makes more sense of the experience we have, and of reality as it impinges upon us, than any other understanding. The fact that the idea of God crops up all over the place is actually direct evidence that human beings need to believe in God, but not direct evidence for the existence of God. It does show that all human beings in every culture seem to have felt inadequate without the notion of God. But the fact that we have often ended up with different views of God again doesn't disprove the reality of God at all, any more than the fact that human beings ended up using very different languages doesn't mean that all language refers to nothing. It doesn't. It means that a lot of our understandings are of course culturally determined. But behind all our belief in God is a faith step anyway. Christians make a major faith step when they say (for which there is no proof), "God is the sort of God who has particularly impinged upon the life of the Jewish people and been shown in Jesus Christ and the life of the Church." That's a faith statement, unavoidable if one is to enter into the Christian tradition.

SWR: *Let's think next about what God is supposed to do -or to have done in the past -if putting it like that is a better way of reflecting popular opinion. I suppose that above all God is seen as creator. "In the beginning God created ...... " I heard a scientist beginning to tell the creation story in a schools' television programme, and he started with the words, "In the beginning there was a random fluctuation in a quantum field .... " Now, surely the scientist carried more conviction than some* *ancient Hebrew mythologist?*

RGJ: Well, he might do or he might not. Christian belief in God as creator is not simply the belief that God started everything off in the beginning. It is the belief that God is the fundamental reality behind all things, now as always, before space-time was itself brought into being. It was God who brought space time into effect, and, if one believes (as I think most people nowadays should believe) that there was a Big Bang sometime or another, perhaps 15 billion years ago, and that at that time all matter was concentrated into a space about the size of a football, then Christians believe that somewhere behind the existence of this extraordinary mass of energy there was the creative activity of God. And when the universe is finished, as one day it might be, there will still be God. So his creative activity is from before time and way on beyond the end of time as well.

SWR: *So the story which conveys is less important than the fact of what it conveys, whether it's the Hebrew story or the Big Bang theory or whatever?*

RGJ: Yes, it so happens that the Hebrew story is particularly powerful and memorable, and is in itself shot through and through with all sorts of insight which the Big Bang account just simply doesn't have. It is a different and in many ways much more profound way of saying, what is it (not was it) all like now? That ancient mythologist was giving us a way of looking at things, complementary to the scientific way.

SWR: *I know we've touched on purpose already to some extent, but I'd like to ask you next whether you think that what God does needs to have purpose. After all, does the universe need to be so serious? Couldn't it be a divine accident? or an experiment? or even a joke? Conscious purpose often seems unnecessary in what science discovers. Things just are: process but not necessarily progress. Working on the assumption that God created the universe -by way of the Big Bang or otherwise - does it necessarily follow that the universe has purpose? And, if so, what is it?*

RGJ: If people like me predicate at the foundation of the whole universe a God who has fashioned it and made reality as it is, then inevitably we are led to believe that there is some purposefulness within it. Why not? But when you say "it's all terribly serious," I don't think belief in God's purpose needs necessarily to be understood as terribly ponderous. It is quite clear that there are lots of things happening, apparently because God so permits or ordains them, which are not of ultimate seriousness. After all, Christians believe that God encourages beauty and music and poetry and all sorts of fascination. God is not deadly serious always, but delights in things. He delights in creativity and art and invention and inspiration and humour and dreams and myths and all the other experience that makes life so intriguing and worthwhile.

SWR: *Let's turn now to the Bible. It seems to be the case that scientific textbooks are out of date within years of publication. Yet our most revered religious book is a collection of writings of varied and sometimes questionable authenticity, works from cultures quite different from our own, written by people living in times of considerable ignorance, stories about others who interpreted life with varying levels of superstition, on original documents which have long since disappeared. Why on earth should anyone consider this collection to be anything other than antiquarian interest?*

RGJ: Because for centuries a whole tradition of religious people have found immense inspiration and encouragement and direction from them. It has helped whole civilisations make sense of life and of the world. That's why the Bible is so significant. The fact that it was written a long long time ago doesn't necessarily mean that it does not carry within it extraordinary openness to God. After all, it's not difficult to assume that people of, say, 2,000 years ago were as open to the reality of God as we are today, or maybe even more so. Their sensing of God's pressure and allure upon their lives is something very significant for us to learn from. I take the Bible in that light. Not as the last word; in no sense a scientific textbook; not even particularly good history; a lot of it is not particularly good history, it is mainly imaginative story telling. And likewise, we would regard many a poet as of profound significance, even though you don't expect poetry to be historically accurate. That's not the point of poetry.

SWR: *Are you talking about what they call the inspiration of the reader?*

RGJ: Yes, I do believe that there is the 'back' of scripture, if you like, an extraordinary fund of spiritual power that the writers were able to draw upon. But so were the first recipients of the writings, and so was the church. After all, the church had the wit to be able to distinguish between some documents that were very odd and which it decided could not be reckoned to be valid scripture, and other documents that clearly carried immense spiritual power and guided Christians in their lives successfully. The Church decided what should be scripture and what should not.

SWR: *Even if we accept that our versions of the New Testament are reasonably close to what the original authors wrote, and even if we make allowances for the cultural influences of the time, don't you think that as modern Christians we often shoot ourselves in the foot by so often dealing with problems and questions by saying, "The Bible says .... " ? Even the Gospels are stuffed with miracle stories which are great obstacles to belief for anyone not brought up in a Christian environment, and those of us who are sympathetic towards Christianity find ourselves so frequently demythologising the Gospels in order to remain within the faith. And even if the Bible does happen to say something about a problem we are facing, the 2,000 -year culture gap surely destroys any reliance we may place upon the views?*

To sum up, wouldn't we do better to say, "Less Bible, more reason"?

RGJ: There's a whole clutch of questions there. I think that for Christian people authority has a fourfold shape to it. We first of all look to the Bible, then we look to the Church, then we look to the whole Christian experience down through the centuries, including our own experience today, and finally our reason which has to make sense of it. All those four together make up Christian authority, not simply the Bible on its own. Simply to say "The Bible says ..... " is not a satisfactory way of expressing authority at all. Moreover, within the Bible itself there are often different understandings of some of the crucial events of Christian belief lying side by side with each other. The Bible doesn't always speak with one voice. It doesn't speak with one voice, for example, about the meaning of Jesus' dying and rising.

There are at least four major understandings of that, lying alongside each other within the covers of the Bible. You can almost take your pick between them, and in different centuries people have. In some centuries one of those has had immense power and seems to have been able to speak to people, and in another century another, and so on. So the Bible is not simply a straightforward textbook of belief: it is not like that, fortunately.

A lot, of course, of the miracle stories are to be understood as attempts of fairly primitive people with a fairly simple understanding of things to make sense of events in a way that today we would find impossible. But there is, running right through Scripture, this profound sense that, when you are in the hands of God, you can never totally explain what is going on in ordinary, everyday, rational, scientific terms. It's always beyond that, greater than that, deeper than that, more profound. So there is always the sense through Scripture, indeed through Christian life today, that the things that happen to us are much more subtle than ordinary, everyday, common sense can cope with.

Now, if one wants to give the term 'miracle' to that -not a very good term, actually -that's OK. There's a great deal, in that sense of miracle, happening to us. We must not try to pretend that life is flat and simple. It isn't at all.

As for the fact that a lot in the Bible is 2,000 years old, and that therefore a great culture gap exists, yes, that's true. But Christian believing is a matter of standing on the shoulders of Christians of the last century, who stood on the shoulders of Christians of the previous one, and so on right back to Abraham, or beyond. There is a great deal of continuity in that. After all, Abraham believed that God was a God who wants to lift you out of your securities and make life an adventure. That runs right through the rest of the Bible and is still something that Christians today must grasp, however vast the culture gap. To do so the culture gap doesn't matter, but basic human fears do.

SWR: *Do you understand the fundamentalist attitude to the Bible? And do you agree that it is quite incompatible with the approach of those who wish to build bridges between science and religion? And wouldn't it be better to have a thoroughly good showdown between the two sides, rather than trying to paper over the cracks?*

RGJ: I do understand that the fundamentalist, not just in the Christian religion but in other religions as well, has a desperate need to believe that faith is all tied up, secure and impregnable, and that mind-cast is likely to be very appealing in a time like ours when there are so many bewildering shifts and changes going on all the time in people's understanding. It's very attractive for the fundamentalist to believe that he has the 'last word' which he must cling on to at all costs. I do understand that and sympathise with it. I don't like the way many modern theologians tend to 'pooh pooh' the fundamentalist. I understand that in some aspects of our lives almost all of us need to have some certainties that we can cling on to at all costs.

Now, the great problem with fundamentalism is, I think, two-fold. The first is that fundamentalists always end up being cruel. That's a terrible indictment. You get fundamentalist Christians who end up being cruel to other Christians. That's the trouble with them. They are intolerant, indeed brutal. Likewise fundamentalist Muslims, Shiite Muslims, are quite cruel and destructive of others, arrogant. So there is that streak in fundamentalism which is very dangerous, ready even to destroy opponents. Fundamentalists are difficult and often awful people to live with, they are so intolerant. The other part is that fundamentalism, of course, cannot hear what modern science or modern culture says. It has to insulate itself off, whether it is Christian or Buddhist or any other kind of fundamentalism, for that matter. That too is dangerous because it tends to produce the split mind, a sort of religious schizophrenia, and that is unhealthy, just as the mental disease schizophrenia tears people apart. It actually looks too much to the past, and narrows the Holy Spirit.

I don't think, however, one can have what you term a showdown with it. In many churches today one has the discussion going on between fundamentalists and other more liberal Christians. But that has always been the case. Think of New Testament times. There were fundamentalists then, and St. Paul had to live with them. They gave him a rough time too. In effect St. Paul is saying, "Well, dear brothers, we've got to learn to love another, even though we knock each other about like this." So, it's nothing new. Christians have always had this struggle going on. Certainly fundamentalism can't cope with modern science, can't make sense of it, nor many other aspects of modern culture. Nor can they make much sense of, let us say, the Women's Liberation Movement.

Fundamentalism is totally at a loss when it is faced with that, and therefore ends up being cruel to women. So I'm unhappy about fundamentalism because it is exclusive and cruel and so blatantly unlike Jesus Christ.

SWR: *It can be argued that, when we come to consider we human beings in our setting in the vast universe, we find theology at its most absurd. Our size is minute, our life is fleeting, our power is minuscule. Yet we insist on picking out isolated phrases from the Bible and and saying that we are made in God's image (whatever that means) and that he has made us little less than gods. So, what is man? And isn't there an unChristian lack of humility in our theologising about people?*

RGJ: Yes, there is. There is a major move in modern theology which says we must now begin to respect the whole of creation, the whole universe, as that which God loves and brings into being and cares for, not just mankind. And that's now beginning to reverberate very creatively in a great deal of modern theology. I'm sure the World Council of Churches' programme on Justice, Peace and the Integrity of Creation -an awkward title - has helped, as has what you might call the 'revolt of nature'. Everybody is beginning to realise that we are damaging the universe and the natural order in a dreadful way, and so we've go to do a massive and quick re-think of our understanding of nature. Theology is doing that fast, in some ways faster than some of the relevant branches of science. In the past the phrase 'being made in the image of God' has justified Christians making out that the whole universe exists simply for our benefit. That is being massively re-thought in today's theology, and is one of the very healthy signs of current Christian reflection.

SWR: *It seems that the relationship between God and human beings is an important aspect of Christian theology, that an important part of any relationship is communication, and that the way people communicate with God is primarily through prayer. In fact, prayer is an activity which is found in nearly all religious practice. Now, prayers of thanksgiving, adoration and confession require no answer and are therefore untestable. Prayers of intercession and petition on the other hand suggest that we expect God to do something. The evidence about responses to prayer, however, is negative if not utterly inconclusive. It is not enough to suggest that God might be saying 'no' or 'wait'. So is communication with God merely a human delusion? Can prayer be tested? If not, why bother?*

RGJ: You can't test prayer, any more than you can construct experiments to prove the existence of God. So, necessarily, we can't prove that prayer in any sense 'works'. In any case, the word 'prayer' tends to be used in rather a narrow way. Most people think that, when you talk about prayer, you are talking about actually saying something to God. A lot of people's actual living with God is not just necessarily saying things to him, but responding right through the fibre of one's being to the sheer wonder of life. In gratitude we respond to the beauty of the world and to all sorts of inspiration that we get day by day, responding with appropriate delight and activity and creativity. All of that is part of our way of living with and for God. As is our way of trying trying to help other people, to communicate with others, to do good. That is all part of our service to God. And if you ask whether it does any good or whether it makes any difference, it's a bit like asking whether it makes any difference if a poet composes a poem. What we should do is to thank God that the poet composes a poem, thank God the musician composes a beautiful piece of music. You don't argue about whether the poem or the music is going to do a lot of good. You just simply rejoice in it.

So our awareness of God is of that character, rather than a business of asking God to get certain mechanisms going in the world and then being able to check whether or not they have happened. What is true to a great deal of experience is that to try to live respondingly to God is very exciting, very fulfilling, and enriches one's life. That's a subjective judgement, and has to be. For me it is abundantly true.

SWR: *Science's explanation of the origin of life in general, and of human beings in particular, might still have a few gaps in it, but is reasonably complete and convincing. Explanations of the rise of religion in terms of answering human needs are also quite reasonable -prenatal experience, inherited innate fears, coping with death, and so on. Wouldn't it be better to try to build a mature attitude to life on these foundations rather than rely on what may be regarded as the religious superstitions of the past?*

RGJ: I don't think it is a question of your doing one or the other, relying on scientific knowledge or religious superstition. In actual experience many of the so-called explanations from the past are in a way helpful and are in no way superstitious. So is a great deal of modern awareness of God all helpful in trying to construct a picture of how it is God is at work with us. So, for example, the recent work of the Sir Alister Hardy's Institute in Oxford, the Institute of Religious Experience, is very fascinating.

It shows that about 65% of English people at the moment claim to have some sort of religious experience, an extraordinarily high figure. They confess to an experience of being in a world which has a transcendent character to it, where there's more than meets the eye, where we often experience being in the grip of a power which is much greater than we are, or than human mechanisms suggest.

Now, I can quite see that it is legitimate for many people to say, "Look, with this widespread awareness there must be more to life than simply the everyday and the commonsensical." They might well link that with all sorts of presumed psychological needs, which also help build up a picture of how it is that God is working with us. So it's not quite a question of one or the other. Interestingly, I notice a very good, very convincing, very well-written theological book, John Taylor's "The Christlike God", starts off by referring to all this vast experience that Hardy has dug up, and then goes on to say how this links up with the experience of people from primeval times up to now, and then shows how Christian belief in Jesus is somehow at the centre of all that and makes the best sense of it.

SWR: *It seems that the impetus which created Christianity and on which much of our theology stands is what we call the resurrection of Jesus. But it is contrary to what we normally experience, and it is impossible to test or repeat it. Furthermore, the idea of life after death often seems more of a threat than a promise, and it would be more comforting to slip into oblivion. Can there be 'unique' events, such as the resurrection of Jesus? And do we really need to believe in life after death to be Christians?*

RGJ: There can be unique events. In a way every event is unique. You are a unique person, so am I, no one else is quite like us. The universe is actually made up of an incredible number of unique events. I notice that scientists nowadays talk about 'singularities', which is just a pompous name for highly unique events. The Big Bang itself was a singularity, a unique event in the history of our universe. So unique events, unique people, are always on the go. Therefore, to suggest that, because the resurrection of Jesus was unique, it may not actually be legitimately talked about or predicated seems to me to be nonsense and most unscientific. Modern science is built on the assumption that all the time we are experiencing the unique, particularly with people. If we ask whether modern science in some way or other disproves the resurrection, the answer is that it does not and could not.

It helps us to see just how significant a unique event it was, a 'singularity' indeed. If we ask whether the resurrection of Jesus actually makes it more promising that there is something good beyond death, Christian experience says that undoubtedly it does.

Christians have always affirmed that the resurrection of Jesus is the greatest act of positive promise in relation to death that has yet occurred within the history of the universe. I see it like that, and I think most Christians do, even if we are slightly disagreed as to exactly what happened. We must be open enough to acknowledge some difficulty as to exactly what happened, partly because it was a long time ago, partly as we haven't got sophisticated records. We must accept some degree of uncertainty. I don't know what went on in the empty tomb, or whether there were angels, or whether the garments were put in a certain way or not, or whether the bones of Jesus are still somewhere or other. No one knows, we can't know. But that doesn't strike me as being terribly important in the modern debate which is raging among theologians. I notice that David Jenkins, who is at the heart of that debate, keeps saying it is not an important debate. What matters is that Jesus was raised, a singular act of God.

Undoubtedly, there are some Christians who are completely agnostic about the after-life, and one respects them. For myself, I think that Christian faith does lead clearly into a notion of an after-life as being the fulfilment with Christ, but I have much sympathy for Christian people who can't easily take that step.

SWR: *Religion seems pretty pointless if our religious beliefs do not affect the way we act. Yet much of the world's misery has been caused, and no doubt will continue to be caused, by people who claim to be acting under the inspiration of religious faith. That applies in the laboratory as well as* *the battlefield. How can theology help us to sort out the good from the bad?*

RGJ: Right from New Testament times there have been two general tests set out, they lie alongside each other, as to how one knows whether or not something is of God. One test is whether a particular movement or particular teaching acknowledges that Jesus is the clearest window we have into God. The other is whether it ends by enhancing human beings, by producing love, by doing good, by promoting human flourishing. These two tests are Siamese twins that operate in the New Testament. They are very good tests, and they show that a great deal of religious behaviour has been absolutely dreadful, whilst much has been superb. The bad side is partly because most people reckon that it is only religious faith that is worth dying for, and therefore worth fighting for. That's why religious wars have been so absolutely bloody and horrible, and people have thrown themselves into them with such vigour, because in the end your faith is the most important thing. It ought to rouse your passions. So it's not surprising that it has caused the most appalling wars. It is such an overall motivating power in people's lives. And if religion had never caused anyone to fight, one would begin to say that there was something wrong with it! So, of course, there has been a lot of evil masquerading under the name of faith. But nevertheless the test as to whether or not it promotes genuine human flourishing and loving and caring, and has at the heart respect for Jesus, seems to me to be the test we still live with today. Mind you, when that test is applied to my life, it makes me squirm a bit. It's a hard test to live under, and one which fills me with shame. So we don't talk about it glibly, for we too live under that judgement.

REFLECTIONS on Beauty in Science

Mr. Rowland D. Budgen

It is no surprise to discover that many school children find some subjects easier to learn than others. Science subjects are generally found easier to learn by those who have a real understanding of them, than by pupils who try to rely on memory but understand little. This results in a steady market for the private tutor who can provide that vital understanding for those who have learnt all that their teachers have told them, but are unable to use that knowledge to answer examination questions or apply it to real situations.

The most effective way of approaching this problem seems to be to draw the pupil's attention to the patterns in the subject. The beauty which emerges as a result greatly enhances the appreciation of the subject, not only instilling an understanding of it, but also enthralling the pupil by its discovery.

Giving examples of these patterns will undoubtedly result in comments that the best ones have been omitted; but consider the following:

1. The study of electric circuits is made much easier for younger children by looking at the behaviour of water circuits. Later on the picture may be extended to the "magnetic circuit".

2. Electricity, magnetism and motion often come together, and are always mutually at right angles. It is not surprising therefore that motors, generators and the wave properties of light are often mentioned in the same sentence.

3. The mathematical procedures required to describe the charging and discharging of a capacitor are identical to those used to describe radioactive decay.

4. Patterns can often be found in sets of related expressions, the speeds of waves in different media and the calculation of many forms of energy being examples.

Creation is the work of a God of beauty. Not only did he create man in his own image, he left the imprints of his character for all who look to find.

A Study Plan for Discussion Groups

It is our hope that readers of this book will find the opportunity to discuss the issues raised in it.

We have found in the past that our publications have been used as the basis for discussion in Fellowship Groups of many kinds. So it has been our custom to include a Study Plan for Discussion Groups, suggesting a break-down of the material, offering stimulus passages from the Bible, and setting a number of questions to get the conversation going.

We trust that the Study Plan which follows will continue to fulfil this useful function.

Session 1

Subject: Knowledge

Bible Passages: John 1:14-18; I Corinthians 13:8-13

Other Reading: Dr. Wilkinson's Lecture

Questions:

1. Is it reasonable to expect that human beings can ever have any absolutely certain knowledge of the environment in which we exist? If so, what kind of knowledge?

2. What do you understand the phrase 'a religious experience' to mean, bearing in mind that over 60% of people are said to have had one?

3. "Science is characterised by its humility before the facts." Are there ways in which that could be said of religion too?

Session 2

Subject: Life

Bible Passages John 1: 1-5; II Corinthians 5 :16-19

Questions:

1. Though many scientific answers to the puzzle of 'what is life?' have been found in recent years, do you think that 'life' continues in any sense to be a mystery?

2. Does detailed biological knowledge about how life begins make it any easier or more difficult for you to believe that God is involved in the process?

3. Do you see any moral problem in the use of genetic engineering
(a) to overcome genetic diseases?

or

(b) to create a new form of living creature?

Session 3

Subject: Thought

Bible Passages: Psalm 8:1-9; Colossians 3: 1-15

Other Reading: Dr. Sloper's Lecture

Questions:

1. Careful scientific study can sometimes enable you to see patterns which you could not see before. Does the same apply to Bible study? How do you distinguish between patterns which were in the original author's mind and those which you impose on the text from your own mind?

2. If personality can be changed by chemical or surgical action on the brain, does it make sense to talk about making 'better people' by those means?

3. I live inside my brain; but I am more than the brain, and I am more than my mind; so what am I?

Session 4

Subject: Psychology

Bible Passages: Acts 2: 14-21; Revelation 1: 9-20

Other Reading: Professor Booth's Lecture

Questions:

1. "God knows the truth; conflicts of view are our problem." What factors can we bring into the process of reconciling people with different views? And how would they know the truth when they found it?

2. How would you distinguish between a hallucination and a vision? If it could be shown that a vision was provoked by some chemical deficiency or excess in the brain, would that nullify the value of the vision's religious message?

3. "The soul is the dynamic within our intentional and involuntary behaviour, not the immortal self, the seat of consciousness, or the 'ghost in the machine' variously understood by the Medieval Church, the Renaissance foundationalists and their followers to this day." Does that definition fit comfortably with your present understanding of 'soul'? If not, what would you wish to add or qualify?

Session 5

Subject: Beauty

Bible Passages: Proverbs 8: 1-11; I Corinthians 2: 1-9

Other Reading: Rt. Rev. Richard Harries' Lecture

Questions:

1. Is the beauty of the natural world enough in itself to turn any human being's thoughts to God?

2. In what ways to you find music a particularly apt analogy for understanding the work of God in creation?

3. What makes a Church building beautiful? Are beautiful objects a help or a distraction in worship in a Church?

Session 6

Subject: Spirit

Bible Passages: Ecclesiates 3: 16-22;
Revelation 21: 1-4 & 22-26

Other Reading: Professor Young's Lecture

Questions:

1. "We have a profound hunch that human existence is more significant than the cycle of birth and natural decay. But that significance rests in God." What do you understand by this statement?

2. What meaning might the word 'salvation' have for the cosmos as a whole? Do Paul's ideas in Romans 8 give an answer to that question?

3. In what way(s) does Jesus have cosmic, universal significance?

Session 7

Subject: Theology

Bible Passages: John 17: 6-19; II Timothy 3: 14-17

Other Reading: Rev. David Winter's Sermon
Dr Jones' Conversation

Questions:

1. How do you react to the idea that we are living in a society which glories in the cult of ugliness, " .... not just in music and art, but in clothing, in language, in what one might call...'manners'"?

2. How can you hold together a high view of the Bible with an acceptance of the broad findings of Biblical criticism?

3. What do you understand by the idea that human beings are made "in the image of God"?

Personnel at the 1993 Conference

Mr Leslie A. Abbotts,
F.R.I.C.S, F.B.I.M.
Quantity Surveyor - retired

Mrs Alison Abbotts,
A.L.C.M.
Teacher

Mrs Paula Aldersley
Initiative Secretary (Plymouth)

Mr Paul Aldersley
Administrator - Plymouth Y.M.C.A.

Mr Maurice Ayre,
C.Eng., M.I.E.E., F.B.I.M.
Manager - retired

Mr John Barnes, M.Inst.C.E.
Civil Engineer

Mrs Hilary Barratt
Dance Movement Therapist
Consultation Hostess

Mr John Barratt, LL.M.
Management Consultant
Initiative Chairman

Mrs Margaret Barrett
Initiative Secretary

Mr Frank G. Beetham,
M.A.
Education Officer - retired

Rev. Dr. Paul A. Beetham,
B.A., B.Sc., Ph.D.
Minister

Mrs Judith Binks
R.E. Teacher, Farmington Fellow

Miss Dorothy Bland,
B.A.
Teacher -retired

Professor David Booth, M.A.,
Ph.D., D.Sc., C.Psychol., F.B.Ps.S.
School of Psychology of the
University of Birmingham
Consultation Lecturer

Miss Wendy Boundy
Student

Mr Robert Brenchley, B.Sc.
Hostel Support Worker

Mr Alan Bristow
Architect

Mrs Stella Bristow
Secretary - Network
Division of Ministries,
Methodist Church

Mr Rowland Budgen,
M.Phil., B.Ed., F.I.M.L.S.,
M.I.Biol.
Physics Teacher

Rev. David M. Caink
Minister

Rev. Dr. John Cameron
Parish Minister

Mrs Myrle Cannell
Librarian - retired
Initiative Bookstall Steward

Mr Peter Cannell, D.L.C.,
F.C.I.P.S.
Consultant
Initiative Treasurer

Dr. Eric I. Chappell, B.Sc., M.Sc.,
Ph.D., C.Chem., F.R.S.C.
Educationalist - retired

Rev. Graham O. Coleman
Minister

Mr Maurice R. Coleman, C.Eng.,
M.I.Mech.E.
Chartered Engineer

Mr Leslie E. Collins, B.Sc.,
C.Eng., M.I.E.E., A.M.B.I.M.
Consulting Engineer - retired

Mrs Marie Collins
Housewife

Mr Tom Corlett, M.A.,
Statistical Consultant

Mr Michael J. Cottrell, G.I.Fire E.
Fire Officer - retired

Mr Richard G. Courtney, B.A.
Material Scientist

Rev. Pam Cram, B.A.
Minister

Rev. Michael Crowther-Green
Minister

Mr John Davenport
Local Government Officer -retired

Rev. A. Ronald Dyer, M.A., B.A.
Minister

Mr R. Edwards, B.Sc.
Retired

Miss Ena W. Evans, B.Sc.
Headmistress

Mr Michael Eve, B.Sc.
Teacher

Dr. K. Bertie Everard, M.A., B.Sc., D.Phil., F.R.S.A., F.I.T.D.
Management Consultant

Mr H.R.R. Fitall, I.Eng.,. F.R.S.A.
Consultant

Mr Eddie Fowler
Accountant

Dr. Alan J. Fudge, B.Sc., Ph.D., C.Chem.
Nuclear Research Scientist

Professor Alec Garner, M.D, Ph.D., F.R.C.P., F.R.C.Path., F.C.Ophth.
Pathologist

Mrs Muriel Glithero
Housewife
Consultation Hostess

Mr Ron Glithero, B.A., B.D.
Lecturer - retired
Initiative Administrator

Mr Colin S. Goodman
Headmaster - retired

Dr. David Gowland, B.A., Ph.D.
University Lecturer

Mrs H. Margaret Gowland
Teacher - retired
Initiative President

Miss Rachel Hadley
Student

Rev. Thomas Hall
Minister

The Rt. Rev. Richard Harries, M.A.
Bishop of Oxford
Consultation Lecturer

Mr Peter Haskins, B.Ed., Dip.A.S.
Teaching Assistant

Dr. Richard Hooker, B.Sc., Ph.D.
Forensic Scientist
Young People's Steward

Mr T. Herbert Hopper, M.R.Pharm.S.
District Pharmaceutical Officer - retired

Mrs Patricia Hughes
Former Teacher
Consultation Hostess

Rev. Harold Langham
Minister

Mrs Gwyneth Little, B.A.
Teacher

Rev. Joyce Lynn, M.I.P.M.
Minister

Mr James Lynn
Health Service Administrator - retired

Rev. James Mack, B.D.
Minister

Mr Bernard E. Martin
Environmental Health Officer

Mr Maurice Metcalfe
Retired

Professor Andrew Miller, M.A.,B.Sc., Ph.D., F.R.S.E.
Head of the Department of Biochemistry of Edinburgh University
Consultation Lecturer

Mr Andrew Moore
Student

Mr Ian Murray
Mechanical Engineer

Mr Michael F. Nance, B.Sc., C.Chem., M.R.S.C.
Industrial Scientist - retired

Mrs Eileen Nish
Receptionist
Consultation Hostess

Mr Norman M. Parkin, B.A., C.Eng., M.I.Mech.E., M.I.I.M.
Industrial Manager - retired

Mr David Peck, B.Sc.,
Science Teacher

Mr John S. Pocock, M.B.E., B.Sc., C.Eng., M.I.C.E., M.I.W.E.M.
Chartered Engineer - retired

Mrs Christine E. Rayner, B.A.
Teacher

Mrs A. Joan Roebuck
Student

Rev. Stuart W. Roebuck, B.D., F.C.I.I.
School Chaplain
Initiative Editor

Dr. Geoffrey T. Rogers, M.A., Ph.D., Sc.D., C.Chem., F.R.S.C.
Biophysical Chemistry research - retired

Dr. John Sloper, M.A., D.Phil., B.M., B.Ch., F.R.C.S.
Senior Registrar of the Eye Department, University of Nottingham
Consultation Lecturer

Mr John F. Southey, M.A.
Agricultural Biologist - retired

Mrs Dorothy Speed
Secretary/Teacher - retired

Rev. W. Norman Stainer-Smith
Minister

Rev. Roy A. Stent
Minister

Mr Michael Taylor
Editor of the Methodist Recorder

Mr Arthur Trafford
Patents Officer - retired

Mrs Joan Trafford
Teacher - retired

Mr. Charles D. Ward,
B.Sc., B.A.
Chemist/ Computer Systems Analyst

Mrs D. Mary Ward
Secretary

Mr Barry Weetman
Regional Writer, Methodist Recorder

Mr Edward Wilkins
Farmer

Mrs Alison Wilkinson
Teacher

Rev. Dr. David A. Wilkinson,
B.Sc., Ph.D., B.A., F.R.A.S.
Chaplain to the University of Liverpool
Consultation Lecturer

Dr. Paul R. Williams,
Ph.D., B.Sc., D.L.C., F.Inst.P., Ch.Phys.
Director of the Rutherford Appleton Laboratory

Mr John H. Willmer, O.B.E., F.R.Ag.S.
Farmer

Rev. Dr. Kenneth B. Wilson,
M.A., M.Litt., Ph.D.
Principal of Westminster College

Rev. David Winter, B.A.
Former Head of BBC Religious Broadcasting, Parish Priest
Consultation Preacher

Dr. John K. Wright,
O.B.E., M.A., Sc.D., M.I.E.E., C.Eng., F.Inst.P., C.Phys.
Director of Health and Safety for Nuclear Electric - retired

Rev. Martin H. Yeomans, M.A.
Minister

Professor Rev. Frances M. Young,
B.A, M.A., Ph.D.
Professor of Theology at the
University of Birmingham
Consultation Lecturer

Printed by
Jiffy Print, King St. Luton
(0582) 20326